DATA
LITERACY

A User's Guide

SAGE was founded in 1965 by Sara Miller McCune to support the dissemination of usable knowledge by publishing innovative and high-quality research and teaching content. Today, we publish more than 750 journals, including those of more than 300 learned societies, more than 800 new books per year, and a growing range of library products including archives, data, case studies, reports, conference highlights, and video. SAGE remains majority-owned by our founder, and after Sara's lifetime will become owned by a charitable trust that secures our continued independence.

Los Angeles | London | Washington DC | New Delhi | Singapore | Boston

DATA
LITERACY

A User's Guide

David Herzog
Missouri School of Journalism

Los Angeles | London | New Delhi
Singapore | Washington DC | Boston

Los Angeles | London | New Delhi
Singapore | Washington DC | Boston

FOR INFORMATION:

SAGE Publications, Inc.
2455 Teller Road
Thousand Oaks, California 91320
E-mail: order@sagepub.com

SAGE Publications Ltd.
1 Oliver's Yard
55 City Road
London, EC1Y 1SP
United Kingdom

SAGE Publications India Pvt. Ltd.
B 1/I 1 Mohan Cooperative Industrial Area
Mathura Road, New Delhi 110 044
India

SAGE Publications Asia-Pacific Pte. Ltd.
3 Church Street
#10–04 Samsung Hub
Singapore 049483

Printed in the United States of America

Cataloging-in-publication data is available for this title from the Library of Congress.

ISBN 978-1-4833-3346-5

This book is printed on acid-free paper.

Publisher: Matthew Byrnie
Digital Content Editor: Gabrielle Piccininni
Editorial Assistant: Janae Masnovi
Copy Editor: Alison Hope
Typesetter: Hurix Systems Pvt. Ltd.
Proofreader: Jennifer Grubba
Indexer: Michael Ferreira
Cover Designer: Anupama Krishan
Marketing Manager: Liz Thornton

SUSTAINABLE FORESTRY INITIATIVE
Certified Chain of Custody
Promoting Sustainable Forestry
www.sfiprogram.org
SFI-01268
SFI label applies to text stock

15 16 17 18 19 10 9 8 7 6 5 4 3 2 1

Brief Contents

Section V. Visualizing data 143

Detailed Contents

Preface: In praise of data literacy

W e're living in an age awash in data, data that are used to make critical decisions in all aspects of our lives: in education, government, economics, public safety, politics, international development, health care, marketing and more. Yet, to many of us, understanding and analyzing data is a dark art that we'd rather leave to the "experts." We'd rather say, "In data we trust."

However, if we choose that path, we do so at our peril.

My desire to write this book developed around 2010, when the tech, business and popular media were mesmerized with all things data. You couldn't go one day without reading, on the Web, reports about how government open-data portals, social-media analytics, big data or data scientists were going to change the world. Only rarely did these reports mention any pitfalls or shortcomings that lurk inside data, potential traps that I'm familiar with from more than two decades of experience as a journalist and educator.

Two events later underscored the need for us to get beyond the hype and really understand data.

First, Nate Silver, then a blogger for *The New York Times,* predicted that President Barack Obama would handily win reelection in 2012. Silver based his prediction on the careful analysis of polling data from all 50 states. Before the election, many pundits, politicians and campaign operatives had assailed Silver, saying that the race was really too close to call. Not only was Silver correct about the strength of Obama's victory, but the blogger had also accurately predicted the contests in all of the states.

Then came the revelation in the spring of 2013 that two Harvard economists had erred in making calculations for an influential study about federal government debt. In the study, the economists had concluded that economic growth plunges when debt exceeds 90 percent of gross domestic product. The study was treated as authoritative in news reports. Elected officials who opposed increased public spending used it to bolster their positions. However, another team of economists later reviewed the data behind the study and revealed their shortcomings, which included a Microsoft Excel spreadsheet miscalculation.

These diverging examples show how important it is for us to become adept at using data. We need to be data literate.

The goal of this book is to help students develop key data literacy skills and practices. Because every student needs to be data literate, the book is aimed at undergraduates across all disciplines who are enrolled in classes that employ research skills. The book is a guide for navigating our data-rich world, and covers all steps: identifying, obtaining, evaluating, cleaning, analyzing and visualizing data.

There's no shortage of textbooks that will help students learn introductory statistical methods using research data. However, this book is unique in that its goal is to impart fundamental nonscientific research skills that all students should know for their academic and professional careers, using readily available software and government data.

The book takes a distinctive approach by weaving in the background information about data with practical, hands-on lessons. For instance, Chapter 8 details best practices in creating number summaries and comparisons, while Chapters 9 and 10 show how to create those summaries and comparisons using Excel.

The how-to chapters of the book liberally employ screen shots and step-by-step instructions to help students walk through the lessons. In addition, at the end of most chapters there are "On your own" exercises or questions that students can work through for practice. At the end of Chapter 3, students are challenged to uncover three state or local databases that they can download.

To help students and instructors, the author has created easy-to-use data files for the lessons and "On your own" exercises. You can find these on the SAGE Publications website at study.sagepub.com/herzog

This book is structured into five sections. Section I is designed to introduce students to the world of data and how they are created. Section II will help students develop a data state of mind that will allow them to discover databases that are available on the Internet or offline at government agencies. Section III will lead them through the process of learning how to evaluate, understand and clean data. In Section IV, students will learn best practices for analyzing data using Microsoft Excel spreadsheets. Section V focuses on how to create charts using Excel and Google Fusion Tables.

In the end, students will have learned key data literacy skills that will prepare them for the more advanced analytical skills that will come later in their studies.

Acknowledgments

This book carries my name as the author but, truth be told, it is the creation of many. I'd like to thank some of them here.

First and foremost, thanks go to all of the great journalists, educators and students whom I've had the good fortune to learn from since joining the Missouri School of Journalism in 2002. Much of what you read in this book was informed or inspired by them.

Also, I would like to thank my colleagues, past and present, at Investigative Reporters and Editors and the National Institute for Computer-Assisted Reporting, in particular Executive Director Mark Horvit and former Executive Director Brant Houston. At the Missouri School of Journalism, I would like to recognize my dean, R. Dean Mills, and department chair Tom Warhover for their steadfast support over the years.

Madeline Odle, an Honors College student at the university, assisted with research, setting up interviews and reading the book copy with fresh eyes. Her contributions were invaluable and helped improve this book immensely.

I'm grateful for former colleague Charles Davis, now dean at the University of Georgia's Grady College, who connected me with SAGE Publications–CQ Press.

Thanks to SAGE acquisition editor Matt Byrnie and editorial director Charisse Kiino for their enthusiasm about taking on this project. Also, thanks go to SAGE production editors Natalie Cannon and Laura Barrett, assistant editor Gabrielle Piccininni and marketing manager Liz Thornton for their contributions. I am indebted to copy editor Alison Hope for her fine work in getting this book into shape. Thanks also to the following reviewers of the book. I very much appreciate their constructive comments and recommendations:

Jim Bernauer, Robert Morris University in Pennsylvania;

Joseph Hayden, University of Memphis;

Albert May, The George Washington University;

Stephen Siff, Miami University;

and David Valentine, University of Missouri-Truman School of Public Affairs.

Finally, thanks to family and friends who provided support as I've worked on this book. In particular, I'd like to thank my son, Ben, for his patience, especially on those days near deadline when I was distracted with writing.

PUBLISHER'S ACKNOWLEDGMENTS

SAGE gratefully acknowledges the contributions of the following reviewers:

James A. Bernauer, Robert Morris University

Michael Tagler, Ball State in Indiana

David C. Valentine, University of Missouri

WELCOME TO THE WORLD OF DATA

CHAPTER 1

DATA DEFINED

B efore we start exploring our world of data, we need to have a solid grasp of exactly what data are and aren't. This might seem like a technicality that we could ignore, but it's important for us to develop an understanding, one that will prepare us as students or professionals to communicate effectively with others who maintain and share data. If we're able to express what we mean by data, we'll be more effective when we're trying to obtain them from the Internet or by using open-records laws.

The word **data**, of course, is the plural of the Greek word datum, and has been around for centuries. So it is nothing new. However, many people misunderstand and misuse the term data. When people think, talk or write about data, they often are referring to information generically. For instance, they might say, "Those are some interesting data points," or, "Do you have data to back up that claim?" In those cases they really mean, "That's some interesting information," or, "What evidence do you have to back up your claim?" In these cases, they might be referring to information that's stored as text, statistics, tables or even charts.

Dictionaries can help us get closer to the definition of data that we'll use throughout this book. It's true that some dictionaries define data more loosely. Merriam-Webster's (n.d.) primary definition of data is this: "factual information (as measurements or statistics) used as a basis for reasoning, discussion, or calculation." The *Oxford Advanced American Dictionary* (Oxford, n.d.) offers a similar primary definition: "facts or information, especially when examined and used to find out things or to make decisions."

If we read past those primary definitions, though, we get definitions that are more on point. Oxford's secondary definition of data is, "information that is stored by a computer" (Oxford, n.d.). This is correct, but not the whole story. After all, this definition would include any music files, Word documents or photos that you might have stored on your computer. Merriam-Webster gets a wee bit closer with its third definition: "information in numerical form that can be digitally transmitted or processed" (Merriam-Webster, n.d.). Data files can be digitally transmitted over computer networks and processed using programs, because data are composed of bits. **Bits** are the smallest units of computerized data.

None of these definitions nails it for our purposes or those of many professionals who work with data, however. So we will consider data to be any computerized file that uses columns and rows (a tabular structure) to organize data that are represented as text, numbers, dates and the like. In addition, these files can be manipulated using programs like spreadsheets and database managers, and can be transmitted over computer networks. We'll learn more about these types of files soon.

MFG_FIRM_FEI_NUM	LGL_NAME	LINE1_ADRS	LINE2_ADRS	CITY_NAME
3008347634	Agostino Recca Conserve Alimentari Srl	Contrada Santa Maria		Sciacca
3007384564	Banaful & Co.	397 Sk Muhb Road		Chittagong
3004398937	Prince Food Products	Commercial Plot No 2, Main Road 1,	Block B, Section 1, Mi	Dhaka
3007450858	Bangas ltd	Doulatdia,Chuadanga,bgangladesh.		Chuadanga
3008518445	Square Consumer Products	Meril Road	Pabna 6600	Salgaria
3004276258	Barnier	Zia Du Barier	34110 Frontignan	Montpellier
3004276258	Barnier	Zia Du Barier	34110 Frontignan	Montepellier
3004276258	Barnier	Zia Du Barier	34110 Frontignan	Montepellier
3004276258	Barnier	Zia Du Barier	34110 Frontignan	Montepellier
3004276258	Barnier	Zia Du Barier	34110 Frontignan	Montepellier
3004276258	Barnier	Zia Du Barier	34110 Frontignan	Montepellier
3004276258	Barnier	Zia Du Barier	34110 Frontignan	Montepellier
3004276258	Barnier	Zia Du Barier	34110 Frontignan	Montepellier
3004255266	Shanxi Changzhi Yunhai Foreign Trade Meat Co. Ltd	NO.41 Changan Road		Changzhi
3004255266	Shanxi Changzhi Yunhai Foreign Trade Meat Co. Ltd	NO.41 Changan Road		Changzhi
3008356772	Yiyuan Haida Foodstuffs Co Ltd	Lucun Town Yiyuan Countyzibo City		Shandong
3008356772	Yiyuan Haida Foodstuffs Co Ltd	Lucun Town Yiyuan Countyzibo City		Shandong
3004251160	Anhui Fuhuang Chaohu Sanzhen Co. Ltd	Huangglu Town,		Chaohu
3004251160	Anhui Fuhuang Chaohu Sanzhen Co. Ltd	Huangglu Town,		Ciuuliu
3009521500	THIEN MA SEAFOOD CO, LTD - FACTORY 3	2.11E STREET 9, TRA NOC II ZONE	O MON DISTRICT	Ho Chi Minh
3008518445	Square Consumer Products	Meril Road	Pabna 6600	Salgaria
3008518445	Square Consumer Products	Meril Road	Pabna 6600	Salgaria

Source: Food and Drug Administration.

Note: Data in a spreadsheet.

Data files may hold information that's been summarized or aggregated in some way. In this example, these data about bankruptcies filed in U.S. courts have already been summarized by federal court districts, circuits and type of bankruptcy (United States Courts, n.d.a). We can easily read the data in this table and see that, in the federal court district for Massachusetts, 3,207 people and businesses filed for bankruptcy during the first quarter of 2013. Of those, 33 filed for Chapter 11 bankruptcy, in which businesses are allowed to reorganize and continue operating (United States Courts, n.d.b).

The purpose of the Excel file that holds the bankruptcy summaries is to provide meaningful information to people who may not know how to manipulate raw data. Anyone who's able to download this Excel file of summaries can get an understanding of bankruptcy filing activity in this quarter. Think of it as a report, with the information already baked in.

Table F-2.
U.S. Bankruptcy Courts—Business and Nonbusiness Cases Commenced, by Chapter of the Bankruptcy Code, During the Three-Month Period Ending March 31, 2013, Based on Data Current as of March 31, 2013

Circuit and District	Total Filings	Total Chapter 7	Total Chapter 11	Total Chapter 12	Total Chapter 13	Business Filings					Nonbusiness Filings			
						Total	Chapter 7	Chapter 11	Chapter 12	Chapter 13	Total	Chapter 7	Chapter 11	Chapter 13
TOTAL	272,296	189,083	2,345	103	80,737	8,512	5,703	1,990	103	689	263,784	183,380	355	80,048
DC	203	166	3	0	34	11	8	2	0	1	192	158	1	33
1ST	7,988	5,230	101	9	2,648	327	183	84	9	51	7,661	5,047	17	2,597
ME	514	409	5	0	100	35	24	5	0	6	479	385	0	94
MA	3,207	2,553	33	3	618	92	55	22	3	12	3,115	2,498	11	606
NH	869	631	10	0	228	65	36	7	0	22	804	595	3	206
RI	869	752	3	0	114	33	30	2	0	1	836	722	1	113
PR	2,529	885	50	6	1,588	102	38	48	6	10	2,427	847	2	1,578
2ND	11,190	9,131	243	2	1,803	564	283	237	2	31	10,626	8,848	6	1,772
CT	1,728	1,481	29	0	218	90	59	29	0	2	1,638	1,422	0	216
NY, N	2,016	1,576	13	2	425	49	26	13	2	8	1,967	1,550	0	417
NY, E	3,546	3,138	64	0	340	149	79	63	0	3	3,397	3,059	1	337
NY, S	2,246	1,758	125	0	356	219	82	120	0	10	2,027	1,676	5	346
NY, W	1,420	989	12	0	419	50	30	12	0	8	1,370	959	0	411
VT	234	189	0	0	45	7	7	0	0	0	227	182	0	45

Predominant Nature of Debt[1]

Source: United States Courts.

Note: Bankruptcy Court data. This spreadsheet summarizes bankruptcy information by type of filing and federal court district.

Other data files hold information that has not been summarized; these are considered **raw data**. We usually can tell if data are raw because one row contains data about one person, place or thing. With the bankruptcies, a raw data file would provide one row with detailed data about each bankruptcy filed by a business or a person. It would probably have, in the first row, headers to tell us what each column holds.

The snapshot of the city of Seattle Police Department's real-time incident reports provides a great example. Each row in the table represents a police report that an officer took when he or she responded to an incident. As you can see from the headers, the officers record data about the offense type, code, location, date, time and other details.

Source: https://data.seattle.gov/Public-Safety/Seattle-Police-Department-Police-Report-Incident/7ais-f98f.

Note: Seattle Police Department incident data.

Municipalities, counties and states provide data files like these as part of open-government initiatives that have gained momentum during the past several years. Seattle and other cities make data files like these available so citizens and other residents can better understand how government operates. In addition, the city makes these files available in formats that developers can use to build mobile applications and Web applications that display crime locations.

However, to someone who is untrained in the ways of data, this file would be nearly useless. All an untrained person could do is download the incidents file, open it in a spreadsheet program and then scroll through it, looking for information. No one has run any calculations yet, or generated a report.

Still, we usually prefer to get raw data. Raw data afford us more flexibility when it comes to analysis. We can make our own decisions about how to summarize. We could use the file from the Seattle Police Department to determine which block in the city has the greatest number of reported crimes, or the greatest number of reported burglaries. Additionally, raw data make it easier for us to examine our data and test the integrity—or quality—of our data, as we will do later in Chapter 5. For more-sophisticated data users, raw data are better.

In the U.S. Courts System summarized bankruptcy file seen earlier, we lack specific data about the individual cases, so we would be limited in what we could do in our analyses. If we really wanted to perform more-sophisticated analyses, we would have to find raw data online. Failing that, we would need to request the data from the U.S. Courts System.

The data files that we will work with in this book all are considered **secondary data**, or data that are collected by individuals other than ourselves. Some academic disciplines and professions analyze data that they've collected themselves; these are considered **primary data**. Primary data are used heavily in the natural and social sciences, as well as in medicine. Such data are sometimes obtained by the process of sampling, or selecting a subset from the whole population of whatever it is you are studying. As you progress in your academic career, you might work more with primary data.

Here are some illustrations of primary data collection:

- A research psychologist interested in the effectiveness of televised antismoking advertisements enlists subjects to watch the ads. The psychologist collects data about the subjects' reactions by asking a series of questions.
- A medical researcher testing an experimental cancer drug enlists subjects, some of whom get the drug while others get a placebo. The researcher uses blood tests to record white cell counts as a way of assessing the effectiveness of the drug.
- A political polling consultant hired by a candidate running for office uses telephone interviews to ask questions of likely voters about what issues are important to them.

CLIMBING THE PYRAMID

Data are our starting point—the raw material that we use to understand our world better. As such, data sit at the bottom of the data-information-knowledge-wisdom (DIKW) hierarchy. Operations research expert R. L. Ackoff spoke about this hierarchy more than two decades ago (Ackoff, 1989).

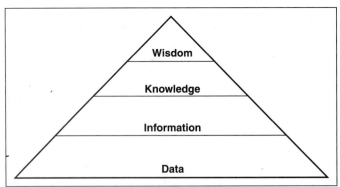

Source: R. L. Ackoff; illustration by author.

Note: The DIKW pyramid.

"The implicit assumption is that data can be used to create information; information can be used to create knowledge, and knowledge can be used to create wisdom," wrote Jennifer Rowley, a professor of marketing and management at the University of Bangor in the United Kingdom (Rowley, 2007, 164.)

A lofty goal, but possible. Here's how the pieces fit together and how we can use them to ascend to the pyramid's peak.

Data, the bottom of the pyramid, are the unprocessed symbols that represent characteristics of objects or people. These data are unorganized and have no meaning or value in isolation (Rowley, 2007). Because data constitute the base of the pyramid and cover a greater area, we can conclude that we are awash in data relative to the other elements in the pyramid. Also, we can see that data serve as the foundation for all of the other levels.

Data can be used to step up to the next level of the pyramid: information. We create information by processing our data using computer programs. For example, we might use a spreadsheet like Microsoft Excel to create totals or averages—descriptive statistics that are more meaningful to us. Or, as we will do later in this book, we might calculate rates or ratios using our data. We could also use database managers like Microsoft Access to perform more-sophisticated analyses, something that is outside the scope of this book. Information is descriptive: it answers questions like Who? What? Where? When? (Rowley, 2007).

After we've generated information, we aim to generate knowledge, which requires us to reflect on the information. Knowledge is created when we take information and turn it into something that can be acted upon (Rowley, 2007). Knowledge helps us and all kinds of professionals—such as teachers, political researchers or business analysts—make better decisions.

As Nate Silver, the founder and editor in chief of ESPN's FiveThirtyEight, put it, "The world has come a long way since the day of the printing press. Information no longer is a scarce commodity; we have more of it than we know what to do with. But relatively little of it is useful. We perceive it selectively, subjectively, and without much self-regard for the distortions that this causes. We think we want information when we really want knowledge" (Silver, 2012, 17).

Helping you learn how to get from data to knowledge is one of the central goals of this book. After you have experience getting from data to knowledge, you may even be able to climb to the peak and attain wisdom. But that takes experience, along with the exercise of values and judgment (Rowley, 2007).

One important point to keep in mind is that working effectively with data requires more than computing. It requires thought and reflection on our own parts. As we climb the pyramid, we rely less on computers and more on our own experiences and thoughts. E. M. Awad and H. M. Ghaziri accounted for this dynamic when they modified Ackoff's

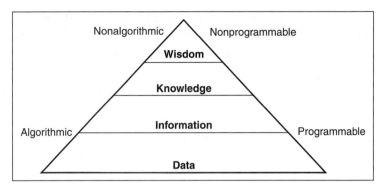

Source: Awad and Ghaziri; illustration by author.

Note: Modified DIKW pyramid.

DIKW pyramid, shown above, for their business knowledge management textbook (Awad and Ghaziri, 2004).

As you can see, this modified pyramid shows that the data at the base can be manipulated by computer programs or **algorithms**—a set of steps for solving a mathematical problem. The steps up to information and knowledge are less reliant on programs and algorithms, and wisdom is not reliant on them at all.

A BRIEF HISTORY OF THE DATA WORLD

With all the recent buzz over open-data portals, big data and data science, it's easy to overlook the roots of data and computing, which stretch back to 20,000 B.C. (The following discussion is based on Wolfram Alpha n.d.) That's when our predecessors invented arithmetic as a tool for calculating numbers of objects. Then, in the years from 2150 to 1700 B.C., they created standards for measurement and multiplication. Later, in 500 B.C., Greek scholar and mystic Pythagoras promoted the idea that the world could be understood by numbers.

Much later, during the Renaissance, Nicole Oresme developed the idea of representing numbers by using graphs, which continue to be important tools for communicating data. Nearly three centuries later, Wilhelm Schickard invented a wooden machine that could add up to six digits.

The Industrial Revolution brought even more innovations that helped create our world of data, including Joseph Marie Jacquard's use of punch cards to control the looms at his weaving mill in France, Charles Babbage's early mechanical computers and Herman Hollerith's use of punch cards to automatically tabulate results from the decennial U.S. census.

The 1940s ushered in the era of digital computers, those that used vacuum tubes to perform calculations on data stored as a series of numbers. In 1963, the American

Standards Association developed the data-encoding system that still dominates computing in the United States. This system is called **ASCII**—short for the American Standard Code for Information Interchange—and allows us to easily share data. ASCII text files are the most portable data files available. The 1970s brought other advances, such as relational **database manager** programs, interactive computing and the first personal computers.

DATA FILE FORMATS

The data files that you store on your computer, whether it's a Mac or PC, can come in hundreds of formats. Audio, video and graphics files all are stored differently and have their own **file extensions** (those characters that come after the file name and period) (FileInfo.com, n.d.). For this book, we'll focus on using just a few different types of data files that we can analyze using **spreadsheet programs** such as Excel or OpenOffice Calc.

Microsoft has two file formats for Excel workbooks, which can hold multiple worksheets. Excel 1997–2003 format workbooks have an **.xls** file extension. A more recent file format, introduced with Office 2007 for Windows, has an **.xlsx** extension and is based on **XML**, or Extensible Markup Language. Microsoft says the XML-formatted files are smaller, more robust and more interoperable than the .xls files (Microsoft Developer Network, n.d.).

Aside from using Excel's native files, we can use files in other formats. Excel and Calc can open OpenDocument spreadsheet format files. The files have an .ods extension and were developed as an XML-based open-source alternative to Excel's proprietary formats. Also, both spreadsheet programs can work with the proprietary **dBASE** database file format. dBASE files have a .dbf extension

Text files are perhaps the most useful format of all because they can be read, processed and exported by all computers and data analysis programs. In the United States, these files are usually encoded with the ASCII characters, making them readable by mainframe computers, servers, Macs and PCs alike. These text files come in two different flavors: **fixed-width** and **delimited**. You can examine both types using a **text editor**, such as **Notepad++**, which is a free and **open-source software** Windows program that's able to handle large files. **TextWrangler** is a good choice for Macs that is also free.

The data inside fixed-width text files already are nicely arranged into columns and rows. The table looks just how we'd expect a data table to look. The following example is a table of aircraft types compiled by the Federal Aviation Administration. Each of the 7,655 lines contains data about one type of aircraft. Eyeballing the file, we might make some solid, educated guesses about where column breaks should go, but we really can't be sure.

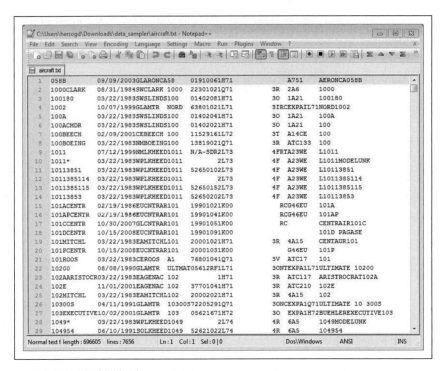

Source: Federal Aviation Administration.

Note: Federal Aviation Administration aircraft data. The data are arranged in columns, which tells us this is a fixed-width text file.

Source: Federal Aviation Administration.

Note: Documentation for FAA aircraft file.

Fortunately, the FAA provides documentation that tells us what the names for the columns should be, and where the breaks go. In this case, we see Model is the name of the first column, and that it is a character column 12 characters wide.

In contrast, delimited text looks like a mess, as you can see from the following earthquake report data released by the U.S. Geological Survey. The data are all smashed together—it looks like a train wreck. However, if you look closely, you will see that commas separate different pieces of data in each row. We call these comma-separated or comma-delimited text files. Data can be delimited by other ASCII characters such as the tab, pipe (|), tilde (~), exclamation point (!) or carat (^). Even though these data look gnarly, they are easier to import than data in a fixed-width file, because computer programs can read the **delimiters** and automatically determine where the column breaks go.

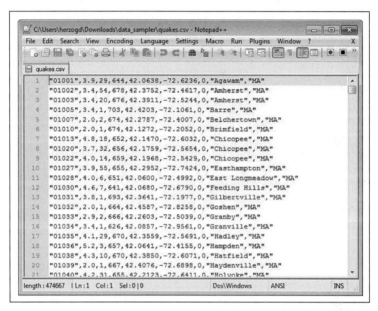

Source: Geological Survey.

Note: A comma-delimited text file. This delimited file uses commas as column separators and double quotation marks to denote text.

There is no convention for specifying extensions with text files, but you will often see .txt, .csv (comma-separated values), .tsv (tab-separated values), .tab, .prn or .dat. If you ever get a text file with an extension that Excel is unable to recognize, simply rename it with one of the extensions it does recognize.

Now that you know what data are, we're going to learn about clues that will help you discover the data you need.

IDENTIFYING AND OBTAINING DATA

CHAPTER 2

CLUES FOR UNCOVERING DATA

One of the big challenges in becoming data literate is being able to quickly identify data and determine which government agency keeps them. If the data are posted on the Internet, we can find and download them. If data are not posted online, we can request them from the agency.

To meet that challenge we need to develop a data state of mind, one that opens our eyes to the proliferation of data online, in government agency mainframes and servers, and in university libraries. After developing a data state of mind—or data antennae—it will be easier for us to see the possibilities. Data are everywhere.

Understanding how and why government agencies process data is a good first step toward developing that data state of mind. Specifically, we'll examine how and why agencies collect, analyze and publish data. To look at it another way, we'll examine the data input and output.

HOW AND WHY AGENCIES COLLECT, ANALYZE AND PUBLISH DATA

Broadly speaking, agencies collect, analyze and publish data for one or more of three primary reasons: (1) they're required to do so by law, (2) agencies believe the data will help them execute their missions or (3) agencies are participating in an open-government effort.

Laws are one of the biggest motivations for state, local or federal government agencies to collect data. Sometimes the laws specifically require the creation of a database. Other times agencies use databases so they can comply with their responsibilities laid out in the laws.

The U.S. Coast Guard's Boating Accident Report Database holds data about recreational accidents reported to state law-enforcement authorities. In the most recent year available, 2012, the Coast Guard recorded 4,515 accidents that killed 651 people and caused 3,000 injuries. The Coast Guard uses the database, which anyone can obtain by making a U.S. Freedom of Information Act request, to track boat accident trends and to generate boating statistics publications that are posted on the Web (Coast Guard, n.d.). In addition, the Coast Guard provides a search interface that allows users to query the database and generate reports in tabular form that they can then export to an Excel spreadsheet.

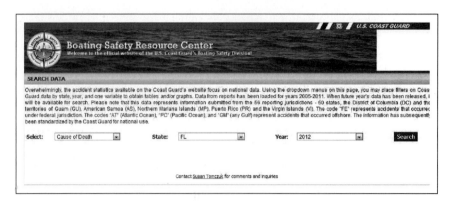

Source: Coast Guard. Retrieved from https://bard.cns-inc.com/Screens/PublicInterface/Report1.aspx.

Note: Boating accident search page. The U.S. Coast Guard allows the public to search its database of recreational boating accidents with this Web form.

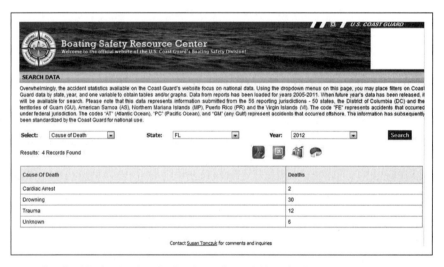

Source: Coast Guard. Retrieved from https://bard.cns-inc.com/Screens/PublicInterface/Report1.aspx.

Note: Cause of death search results for the state of Florida, 2012.

Publishing these data on the Web clearly is a benefit to law enforcement; boating safety advocates, such as the National Safe Boating Council; and members of the public. Regardless of these benefits, the Coast Guard is doing so because of a law. Congress in 1983 passed legislation establishing the State Marine Casualty Reporting System within the U.S. Department of Transportation. The Coast Guard was part of the Department of Transportation and now is part of the Department of Homeland Security.

The law, as amended the next year, says,

(a) The Secretary shall prescribe regulations for a uniform State marine casualty reporting system for vessels. Regulations shall prescribe the casualties to be reported and the manner of reporting. A State shall compile and submit to the Secretary reports, information, and statistics on casualties reported to the State, including information and statistics concerning the number of casualties in which the use of alcohol contributed to the casualty.

(b) The Secretary shall collect, analyze, and publish reports, information, and statistics on marine casualties together with findings and recommendations the Secretary considers appropriate. If a State marine casualty reporting system provides that information derived from casualty reports (except statistical information) may not be publicly disclosed, or otherwise prohibits use by the State or any person in any action or proceeding against a person, the Secretary may use the information provided by the State only in the same way that the State may use the information. (U.S.C. Title 46, 2011)

We can see from the letter of the law that the Department of Transportation was under orders not just to compile these data from state agencies in a consistent format, but also to generate reports and make them public.

Although the law does not give instructions about what data elements need to be collected for the reports, the department later developed regulations that determine when boating accidents must be reported, by whom and within what time frame. In addition, the regulations specify the minimum data that should be collected, including location, time and date, weather and water conditions, the availability and use of personal flotation devices and more (Government Printing Office, 2001a, 2001b).

Another federal database that was created to comply with the law is the U.S. Environmental Protection Agency's Risk Management Plan database. The EPA's RMP database holds data about certain chemicals that are produced, stored or distributed at facilities across the country. These RMPs are supposed to be a tool to help local emergency responders, such as firefighters and paramedics, to better plan for and respond to fires and explosions, like the deadly one at the West Fertilizer Company in the town of West, Texas, in 2013.

The EPA does not post the database online itself: the Right to Know Network, a project of the nonprofit Center for Effective Government in Washington, DC, posts it. Visitors to the RTKNet website can examine data that have already been summarized, such as this chart showing the number of

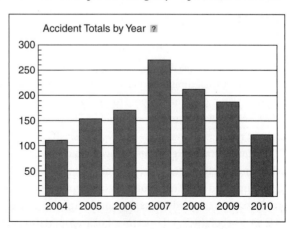

Accident Totals by Year

Source: Risk Management Plan Database. (n.d.). The Right-to-Know Network. Retrieved July 10, 2013, from http://www.rtknet.org/db/rmp/search.

Note: U.S. hazardous chemical accidents by year. The nongovernmental Right to Know Network generates charts using data from the U.S. Environmental Protection Agency.

Facility and parent names

Facility Name [?]: [_____]
Parent Company Name [?]: [_____]
Facility, Parent, Owner or Operator Name [?]: [_____]

Location

City [?]: [_____]
County [?]: [_____]
State [?]: [All -- Entire U.S. ▾]
Zip Code [?]: [_____]
Congressional District [?]: [All -- Entire U.S. ▾]

Other search criteria

Executive Summary Text [?]: [_____] (free text search)
Industry [?]: [All ▾]
(searches all process NAICS codes)
Chemical [?]: [All ▾]

Display options

Level of Detail [?]: [Summary ▾]
Output Type [?]: [Text (HTML) ▾]
Sort order [?]: [By facility name ▾]

[Search] [Clear]

Source: Risk Management Plan Database. (n.d.). The Right-to-Know Network. Retrieved July 10, 2013, from http://www.rtknet .org/db/rmp/search.

Note: Right to Know Network's U.S. Risk Management Plan search screen.

reportable accidents by year. Site visitors can also run more-complicated queries using a form to drill down and get details about particular facilities (Center for Effective Government, n.d.).

Established in 1970 by President Richard Nixon, the EPA is in charge of enforcing federal air, water and ground pollution laws. (In some states, the EPA has delegated duties to state-level agencies.) The RMP database has its roots in the Clean Air Act of 1970, which sought to curtail air pollution caused by urbanization and industrialization.

Twenty years later, President George H. W. Bush signed into law amendments with provisions intended to prevent chemical accidents. The EPA developed rules and required facilities to comply by 1999 (Environmental Protection Agency, n.d.b).

The regulations specify which 77 toxic and 63 flammable substances facility owners must report, and at what threshold quantities. For example, facilities that have 10,000 pounds of anhydrous ammonia must report to the EPA (Chemical Accident Prevention Provisions, 1994). The fertilizer factory in West had 54,000 pounds on hand in June 2011, according to the most recent EPA data on the RTKNet website (Center for Effective Government, n.d.).

In other instances, government agencies create databases on their own initiative, to help them meet their own strategic goals. The National Highway Traffic Safety Administration is supposed to reduce deaths, injuries and economic losses caused by motor vehicle accidents in the United States (National Highway Traffic Safety Administration, n.d.). NHTSA, part of the U.S. Department of Transportation, developed the Fatality Analysis Reporting System database in 1975 as a tool for monitoring fatal traffic accidents across the

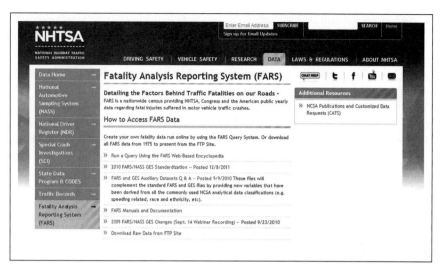

Source: National Highway Traffic Safety Administration. Retrieved from http://www.nhtsa.gov/FARS.

Note: Fatality Analysis Reporting System home page.

country and giving researchers data that they could use to examine the causes. State agencies collect the data about the fatal crashes and then provide them to NHTSA, which compiles FARS and releases the data annually to the public. Transportation planners, safety advocates, journalists and attorneys all have used the data for research. NHTSA itself has used the data over the years to generate dozens of analytical reports available for download.

NHTSA allows site users to query its data using a series of Web forms. More-advanced data users, such as those who have experience using database managers, can download raw data files back to 1975—the inaugural year for the database.

We can see that governments have different motivations for collecting, using and making data public. That's important for us to consider later when we're testing our data, using integrity checks. Our goals for working with the data can differ greatly from the goals of the people inside the agencies that collect them. For instance, we may be interested in determining which industry group's employees contributed the most money to candidates running for governor in our state. However, our state probably records the occupation and employer—but not industry category—of each contributor. That means we won't be able to answer that question without a lot of additional research and changes to our campaign contribution data.

CLUES FROM DATA ENTRY

As we begin to develop a data state of mind, we should keep our eyes open for clues that government agencies are creating databases. Agencies have a multitude of ways to enter data into a database, some of them high tech, others rooted in the paper-bound ways of the 20th century.

We may see government workers collecting data in the field using handheld computers as part of their jobs. For instance, parking enforcement officers in your city and on your campus might be using devices that allow them to enter violation data and to print out, right on the spot, a ticket that looks like a store or ATM receipt. Some units, which look like big, rugged calculators, have number and character buttons for the data entry. Others have touchscreens with styluses. Some even come with GPS receivers so the officers can record the precise location of where a parking violation occurred. In a similar vein, other government agencies, such as fire departments and health departments, have been using tablet devices to input onsite inspection data.

When we see this data collection, we can assume that the data do not stay in the individual handheld unit or tablet. In fact, these data later are transferred to a centralized database that holds all of the inspections.

Likewise, police officers do data entry in the field when they respond to calls from 911 dispatch centers. With the aid of their ruggedized laptop computers mounted next to them in their cruisers, they use templates to enter distinct pieces of data about the report. For instance, an officer might enter data about the location, nature and outcome of an incident, and the name and contact information of any witnesses interviewed at the scene. When the officer has completed the report, he or she can send it to the police department's centralized incident reporting system.

Most data entry, however, is nowhere near as advanced. A lot of data entry is done using paper or Web forms, so we should look for those, too, as clues. It's hard to believe, but a lot of data at government agencies are entered manually. A clerk sits at a computer and keys in data that someone has entered on a paper form. So, if you see someone entering data in a government building, casually ask them what they're doing and about the data they work with. Sometimes government agencies scan their forms and use software to digitally extract the data.

If you're interested in a database, get a copy of the form that's used to feed data into it. Forms tell a lot about what you can expect to find in databases. You should assume that all of the data collected on the form will be entered. You may be incorrect, but you should start with the assumption that more data are available.

Here's a good example of a government form used to collect data. The U.S. Bureau of Alcohol, Tobacco, Firearms and Explosives licenses firearms dealers, which include big box retail, sporting goods and hunting shops. Whenever a federal firearms licensee (or FFL) loses or has firearms stolen, the licensee must report that loss or theft to the ATF's National Tracing Center within 48 hours. The ATF enters the data about the stolen firearms into the database and later searches them when law enforcement agencies want to trace guns that were used in crimes (Bureau of Alcohol, Tobacco, Firearms and Explosives, n.d.).

U.S. Department of Justice	OMB No. 1140-0039 (07/31/2012)
Bureau of Alcohol, Tobacco, Firearms and Explosives	**Federal Firearms Licensee Firearms Inventory Theft/Loss Report**

All entries must be in ink. Please read notices and instructions on reverse carefully before completing this form.

Section A - Federal Firearms Licensee Information

Federal Firearms License Number	Federal Firearms Licensee Telephone Number *(Include area code)*

Trade/Corporate Name

Street Address of Federal Firearms Licensee	City	State
	Zip Code	Telephone Number *(with area code)*

Full Name of Person Making Report

Street Address of Person Making Report	City	State
	Zip Code	Telephone Number *(with area code)*

Section B - Theft/Loss Information

	Date	Time	Description of Incident
Date of Theft/Loss Discovered			☐ Burglary ☐ Robbery
Police Notification			☐ Larceny ☐ Missing Inventory
			ATF Issued Incident Number
ATF Notification			

Name of Local Authority to Whom Reported (For burglary, larceny or robbery, include the police report number and officer/ detective name).

Street Address of Local Authority	Theft Location if Different from FFL Premises		
City	State	Zip Code	City	State	Zip Code

Name and Telephone Number of the ATF Representative Notified *(If this report is the result of an ATF compliance inspection, provide the name and telephone number of the ATF Inspector.)*

Brief Description of Incident *(e.g., How firearms were stolen, etc.)*:

Section C - Description of Firearms

Acquisition Date	Type	Manufacturer	Model	Caliber/ Gauge	Serial Number

Certification

I hereby certify that the information contained in this report is true and correct. I also understand that failure to report the theft or loss of a firearm from my inventory or collection within 48 hours of the discovery of the theft/loss is a violation of 18 U.S.C. § 923(g)(6) punishable as a felony.

Signature of Licensee	Date

ATF Form 3310.11
Revised September 2009

Source: Bureau of Alcohol Tobacco, Firearms and Explosives, Department of Justice. Retrieved from https://www.atf.gov/files/forms/download/atf-f-3310-11.pdf.

Note: Federal form used to report lost or stolen firearms.

The boxes or fields on the form tell us exactly what gets collected. We see details about the FFL, including license number and street address. The form asks for the contact information of the person making the report; details about the theft or loss, including when local police were contacted; type of incident; and a brief description. Also, there's space for data about the firearms stolen or lost, including the manufacturer, model and serial number.

It might be an overstatement to say government agencies love forms, but they certainly do thrive on them. In fact, if you type http://forms.gov in your browser, you'll land at the federal government's portal for forms.

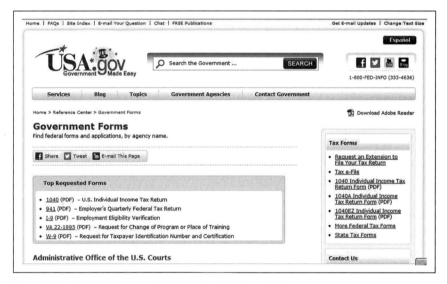

Source: Retrieved from http://www.usa.gov/Topics/Reference-Shelf/forms.shtml.

Note: Website for forms used by federal agencies.

Some of the forms accessible from this portal are Web forms, not documents such as Microsoft Word or Adobe Acrobat files. More agencies, large and small, are employing these online forms to collect data. For example, anyone who wants to have a parade, run or other event using the streets in the city of Columbia, Missouri, must complete the following Web form, then click the Submit button. These data then go from the form into a database administered by the city. The form's URL, which has a .php extension, is our clue to the presence of a database. **PHP** is a programming language that lets Web forms pass data to databases. Also be on the lookout for **.cfm** (Adobe ColdFusion) and **.asp** (Microsoft Active Server Pages), which can also pass data from a Web form to a database. By examining the city's form, we know that it collects data about the person making the request and the nature of the event, such as the time, date and location.

Save for Later	Save & Continue	Cancel Changes			
APPLICANT INFORMATION					
Are you the applicant organizing this event on behalf of another organization? *					
○ Yes ○ No					
APPLICANT CONTACT:	Name: * David Herzog		Phone: *		Cell:
	E-mail Address: david.herzog@gmail.com		*		
MAILING ADDRESS:	Street Address:		*		
	City: *		State: *		Zip: *
SECONDARY CONTACT:	Name:		Phone:		Cell:
	E-mail Address:				
ON SITE CONTACT (if different than applicant):	Name: *				Phone: *
EVENT INFORMATION					
EVENT NAME:				*	
EVENT CATEGORY: *		○ Procession/March ○ Concert/Performance		○ Non-Competitive Athletic Event ○ Neighborhood Block Party	

Source: City of Columbia, Missouri. Retrieved from https://www.gocolumbiamo.com/CMS/special_events/step1.php.

Note: City of Columbia, Missouri, form for parade permit applications.

CLUES FROM REPORTS

So far, we've been looking at how data collection can help us uncover clues about databases. Now we're going to look at how the products of databases, such as reports, can help. Another way of thinking about this is that data collection provides the input, reports provide the output.

As we saw earlier, agencies may collect data to fulfill legal mandates or help them meet strategic goals. The same applies to agencies issuing reports. In addition, executive agencies—at the federal, state or local level— often generate reports using data at the request of the legislative bodies that oversee them.

The Texas Parks and Wildlife Department regulates hunting in the state and issues licenses to hunters. It also collects data about hunting accidents that it

2012
TEXAS HUNTING INCIDENTS ANALYSIS

TEXAS PARKS & WILDLIFE

Source: Texas Department of Parks and Wildlife. Retrieved from http://tpwd .state.tx.us/publications/pwdpubs/media/pwd_rp_k0700_1124_2012.pdf

Note: Texas annual report for hunting accidents.

uses to produce annual reports (Texas Parks and Wildlife Department, n.d.). These reports summarize accidents for the year and, in some cases, provide data from other years for comparison. The summarized tables, like the ones below, provide a good clue that the underlying data for this report came from a database.

EQUIPMENT	Percentage in parentheses (%)			
Rifles	16 (55)	8 (32)	11 (48)	11 (44)
Shotguns	11 (38)	16 (64)	9 (39)	11 (44)
Handguns	2 (7)	1 (4)	2 (9)	3 (12)
Muzzleloader	0	0	0	0
Bow	0	0	1 (4)	0

Source: Texas Department of Parks and Wildlife, Retrieved from http://tpwd.state.tx.us/publications/pwdpubs/media/pwd_rp_k0700_1124_2012.pdf

Note: Table in hunting accidents report.

We get an even stronger indication that these data came out of a database when we arrive at the section that provides details about the individual hunting incidents. (Two fatal accidents from 2012 are shown below.) Each has a header for the date, county, shooter's age, gender, firearm, animal hunted, whether the accident was self-inflicted and whether the shooter had taken a hunters' education course.

2012 FATAL INCIDENTS FIREARM/BOW HUNTING RELATED (A)*
*A. Firearm/Bow & Hunting Related—An accident/incident resulting from the discharge of a firearm or bow while hunting, which causes the injury or death of any person(s).

Date	County	Shooter's Age/Gender	Firearm	Animal Hunted	Self-Inflicted?	Hunter Ed? (Shooter)
4-?	Bexar	36/M	Rifle	Opossum	No	No

Comments: Shooter shot at an opossum after dark and did not see that his friend was in the line of fire.

Prevention: Always point the muzzle in a safe direction; always stay within a safe zone of fire; communicate with hunting companions; know where others are positioned at all times; never fire from behind others; complete hunter education.

11-10	Polk	42/M	Rifle	Deer	No	No

Comments: Shooter was unloading his rifle at the rear of his truck after hunting. Gun discharged through the rear of the vehicle, striking victim in lower back as he sat in the cab of the truck.

Prevention: Always point muzzle in a safe direction; treat every firearm as if it is loaded; handle firearms carefully; complete hunter education.

Source: Texas Department of Parks and Wildlife. Retrieved from http://tpwd.state.tx.us/publications/pwdpubs/media/pwd_rp_k0700_1124_2012.pdf

Note: Detail section of Texas hunting accidents report. This section of the report includes data about each hunting accident reported to the state.

The U.S. Consumer Financial Protection Bureau began operations in 2011, the year after it was established by the Dodd-Frank Wall Street Reform and Consumer Protection Act. Dodd-Frank sought to stem many of the mortgage, credit card and other consumer lending predatory practices in the 2000s. The bureau takes and investigates consumer complaints. Consumers can even use an online form, such as this one, for credit card complaints.

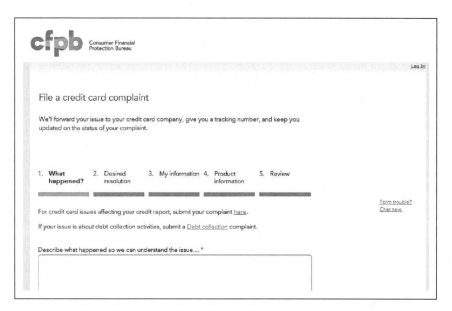

Source: Consumer Financial Protection Bureau. Retrieved from https://help.consumerfinance.gov/app/creditcard/ask.

Note: Consumer Financial Protection Bureau online complaint form.

In the summer of 2013, the CFPB released a 19-page report that provides a snapshot of complaints and how they are handled. The report relies heavily on summarized numbers and charts to communicate data about the complaints. Also, the report tells us that data were derived from a database of the complaints (Consumer Financial Protection Bureau, n.d.a). So no guesses here!

TRICKS TO UNCOVER FORMS AND REPORTS

Finding forms and reports on government websites can be a challenge. Many times, agencies scatter them about rather than provide a centralized home for them, as the federal forms portal strives to do. Fortunately, we can use some Internet sleuthing tricks, using Google Advanced Search.

Point your browser to http://www.google.com/advanced_search and you'll see a user interface that is much busier than the serene, default Google search page. The advanced search allows us to limit our searches to specific websites, document formats or both. So this means we can look for PDF forms on government websites (those having a .gov) domain, or even for forms on the Pennsylvania Department of Education website (education.state.pa.us). Go ahead and enter "form" in the Find pages with . . . all these words box. Then enter "education.state.pa.us" in the Then narrow your results by . . . site or domain box. Now search and look at your results.

Find pages with...		To do this in the search box
all these words:	form	Type the important words: tricolor rat terrier
this exact word or phrase:		Put exact words in quotes: "rat terrier"
any of these words:		Type OR between all the words you want: miniature OR standard
none of these words:		Put a minus sign just before words you don't want: -rodent, -"Jack Russell"
numbers ranging from:	___ to ___	Put 2 periods between the numbers and add a unit of measure: 10..35 lb, $300..$500, 2010..2011

Then narrow your results by...		
language:	any language	Find pages in the language you select.
region:	any region	Find pages published in a particular region.
last update:	anytime	Find pages updated within the time you specify.
site or domain:	education.state.pa.us	Search one site (like wikipedia.org) or limit your results to a domain like .edu, .org or .gov
terms appearing:	anywhere in the page	Search for terms in the whole page, page title, or web address, or links to the page you're looking for.
SafeSearch:	Show most relevant results	Tell SafeSearch whether to filter sexually explicit content.
reading level:	no reading level displayed	Find pages at one reading level or just view the level info.
file type:	any format	Find pages in the format you prefer.
usage rights:	not filtered by license	Find pages you are free to use yourself.

Source: Google search.

Note: Google Advanced Search screen.

You can also use the advanced search to restrict your results to PDF or Word files by using the file type drop-down list.

After you get more experience running advanced searches, you can run them right from the main Google search box by mimicking the syntax that appears after you run the advanced search. For our query, this says, "form site:education.state.pa.us". Google translates that as instructions for it to look for the word "form" anywhere inside the education.state.pa.us domain. So if you want to look for forms on the EPA site, you'd type "form site:epa.gov". To get only PDF forms, try, "form site:epa.gov filetype:pdf".

Now that you are equipped with some tips for developing a data state of mind, we're going to tackle the world of online databases and develop some strategies for locating and downloading them. Being able to find relevant online data and download them is one of the key data literacy skills that you'll need to succeed.

ON YOUR OWN

Choose one of the two federal databases and find the law that led to the creation of the database: U.S. Food and Drug Administration's Operational and Administrative System for Import Support or U.S. Department of Education's Campus Safety and Security database. Cite the law and write a few paragraphs explaining how the law made the database possible.

Every state has an agency whose mission is to collect and disclose political campaign finance data. Identify that agency in your state. Cite and summarize the law that gives the agency the authority to collect these data.

Find a form that a federal, state or local government agency uses to collect data. Specify where you found the form, and include a URL if you downloaded it from the Internet. What data does the agency collect with the form? Try to find a corresponding database online and provide its URL if you are successful.

CHAPTER 3

ONLINE DATABASES

I n a perfect world, we would be able to easily download all of the data that we need from the comfort of our computer keyboards. All government agencies, from the federal down to the local, would post all of their public data on easy-to-find websites that have been well-indexed by search engines. The agencies would make their data available in formats that could be easily opened in our spreadsheet or other analysis and visualization programs. They would also provide copies of any documentation that we'd need to help understand the data, and make sure that the documentation is complete.

That perfect world, of course, does not exist and never will. Although it's impossible to know the exact percentage of data that are available, it's a safe bet that government agencies in general post less than half of their data online, despite the high-profile efforts that are part of the **open government** movement. Agencies may post the data in formats that are difficult to import into—or are too large for—spreadsheet programs. Agencies also may post data without providing the documentation that users need to understand them. There are all kinds of real-world challenges when it comes to finding the right data online and using them effectively.

In this chapter, you will learn effective techniques for quickly finding, understanding and using data sets from government agencies. Because the Internet changes daily, no one can create a list of must-know sites that we'll be able to use ten or even five years from now. So the best approach is to understand how government agencies store data online and adopt the best practices that will help you find what you need in a reasonable amount of time. Also, when you find sites that you'd like to revisit, make sure you bookmark them so you can reference them easily later.

DESTINATION: DATA PORTALS

Government **data portals** have come into vogue with some agencies and members of the public, thanks to the **Government 2.0** or open-government movement. The movement got a big boost in May 2009, when the Obama administration launched Data.gov as a new public destination for federal government data sets. The federal government's effort was in part modeled on efforts of early innovators, such as the D.C. Data Catalog.

Sometimes, data portals can be frustrating to use. Agencies sometimes only link to existing data, or they post only a limited number of data sets that might not be useful.

Besides the federal government, many other government entities have since launched open data portals, such as Chicago; Austin, Texas; Montgomery County, Maryland; and Oregon. Some cities, such as Philadelphia, have partnered with nongovernment organizations to provide portals.

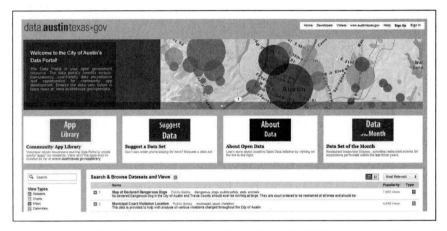

Source: Dangerous and Vicious Dogs. (n.d.). *City of Austin*. Retrieved August 16, 2013, from austintexas.gov/department/dangerous-and-vicious-dogs

Note: Data portal for city of Austin, Texas.

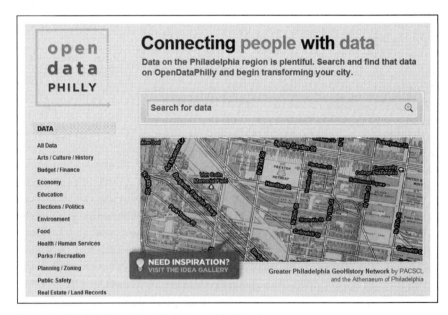

Source: Open Data Philly. Retrieved from http://www.opendataphilly.org/.

Note: OpenDataPhilly portal. The city of Philadelphia partners with a nongovernmental organization to make data available to the public.

Spend some time on the so-called **open data** sites and you notice some similarities in terms of the functions and appearances. That's because two major data-hosting Web platforms—**Socrata** and **CKAN**—dominate. Socrata is a Seattle-based company that sells its open-data platform services to government agencies, numbering at least three dozen in the summer of 2014 (Socrata.com, 2014). CKAN, on the other hand, is an open-source data catalog program that government agencies are allowed to deploy and use with no licensing costs. CKAN was developed by the Open Knowledge Foundation, a nonprofit organization based in the United Kingdom.

Let's explore one of the Socrata-powered sites: data.austintexas.gov. This is the official open data portal of the City of Austin, one that's pretty manageable in terms of size and ease of navigation. The bottom half of the landing page lists data sets posted by the city.

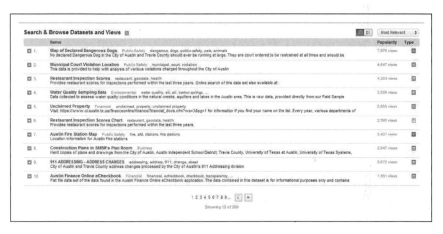

Source: Retrieved from Data.austintexas.gov.

Note: Austin, Texas, data set listing on portal.

After we click on the link for restaurant inspection scores, a list of the inspections appears. Click the About button at the upper right and we get information about the data that will help us understand them better. For instance, we see that the data are for inspections dating back three years, that they have 19,964 rows and that they are updated weekly by the city Health and Human Services Department.

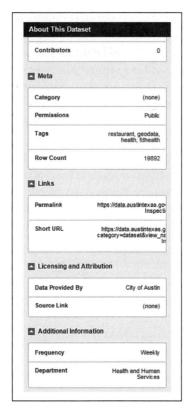

About This Dataset	
Contributors	0
Meta	
Category	(none)
Permissions	Public
Tags	restaurant, geodata, health, fdhealth
Row Count	19692
Links	
Permalink	https://data.austintexas.gov Inspecti
Short URL	https://data.austintexas.g category=dataset&view_na In
Licensing and Attribution	
Data Provided By	City of Austin
Source Link	(none)
Additional Information	
Frequency	Weekly
Department	Health and Human Services

Source: Retrieved from https://data.austintexas.gov/ dataset/Restaurant-Inspection-Scores-Chart/hqa6-stx4

Note: About box on Austin data portal. This box provides some important information about the data provided.

Before we download any data, we need to practice safe computing and document our work: Create a word processing document or text file with the name **Data_Notebook**; this is going to be where we take notes about the data we get and what we do with them. Enter the date, then "Austin restaurant inspections" and the URL "https://data.austintexas.gov/dataset/ Restaurant-Inspection-Scores/ecmv-9xxi". Don't forget to include details about the data, such as the number of rows, time span, update frequency and source.

Now, on to downloading the restaurant inspections file in Excel format onto our computers. Click the Export button, then Download as XLSX to get the most current Excel file format. It may take a few seconds to download the file, depending on your Internet connection and computer processor speed. Look for the downloaded Restaurant_ Inspection_Scores.xlsx file and then open it in Excel. Now we have a copy of the file that we could analyze.

Let's practice safe computing again and make sure we downloaded all of the data: We can see that we downloaded all seven columns. To check the rows, hold the Ctrl and End keys on your keyboard

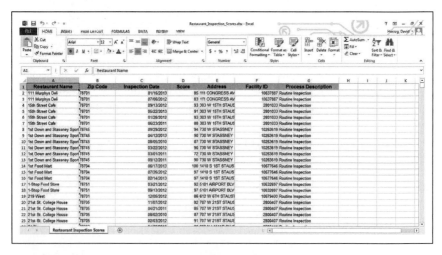

Source: Retrieved from https://data.austintexas.gov/dataset/Restaurant-Inspection-Scores-Chart/hqa6-stx4.

Note: Austin restaurant inspection data downloaded to Excel file.

together at the same time and Excel takes you to the bottom right corner of the spreadsheet (Mac users, use the Command and End keys). We see that we have the same seven columns as at the top, as well as 19,965 rows (one for the headers and 19,964 for the data, just as noted in the About box).

Open data portals also allow us to search. Let's say you're an intern for a local social services agency that wants to better understand affordable housing in Austin. Use the search box at the left of the data.austintexas.gov page to look for affordable housing. The results show us that the city indeed does offer data about affordable housing.

Source: Retrieved from Data.austintexas.gov.
Note: Austin data portal search box.

Now let's go to the data portal for the federal government, Data.gov, which is built on the CKAN open-source platform. There are no data directly on the home page, but users can get to the data via the topic icons or the search box.

Source: Retrieved from Data.gov.
Note: Data.gov home page. The federal government redesigned the home page in 2014 to allow users to more easily search or browse for data.

The easiest point of entry is through the Data tab, which takes us to a list of data sets that we can browse, filter or search. In the summer of 2013, Data.gov cataloged more than 161,000 data sets. That number might seem impressive, but it is a little deceptive and overstates the real number. Many of the data sets that Data.gov links to are extracts of larger databases. For example, the EPA provides links to download Toxic Release Inventory data by state (or federal territory) and year. So the EPA considers the 2009 TRI data for Rhode Island as one data set, even though those data are part of a national database covering many years.

One of the best ways to look for data is to use the powerful filtering tools that are part of CKAN. On the left sidebar of the data set page we can filter by data set type, tags, formats, groups, organizations (or specific agencies) and community categories. We can add filters to further zero in on the data we want. Click on Federal Highway Administration in the Organization Filter and get just the data sets posted by that division of the U.S. Department of Transportation. Data.gov updates your results, showing you the new number and

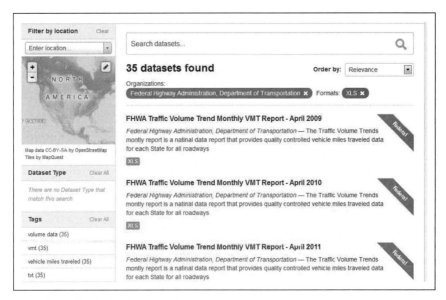

Source: Retrieved from http://catalog.data.gov/dataset.

Note: Search results for Excel files from the Federal Highway Administration on Data.gov.

that you have filtered for the FHWA. Filter more by picking XLS for Excel under the formats filter. The number of results is even smaller and you now have two filters displayed.

Clear the filters by clicking the Xs next to them both.

Searching is pretty easy, too. Just type a search term in the search box and then click on the magnifying glass and you'll get data sets that meet your criteria. At this point you can also apply filters. Let's say we want to find data that might tell us about the declared disasters that have occurred in our state. So go ahead and filter for just data that come from the Federal Emergency Management Agency, which is part of the U.S. Department of Homeland Security. Some of these data, including the Excel file of declared disasters, could be promising.

STATISTICAL STOCKPILES

Another great way to learn more about online data is to tap into the websites of government agencies whose mission is to provide statistical data. On the federal level, this includes the Census Bureau, the Bureau of Justice Statistics, the Bureau of Labor Statistics, the National Center for Education Statistics and the Bureau of Transportation Statistics. On the state level, you might find similar agencies, such as the Missouri Economic Research and Information Center.

The U.S. Census Bureau is one of the biggest data providers in federal government. In fact, its mission is to provide quality data about people and the economy. Many of us know the Census Bureau because of the **decennial census**, which is an attempt every ten years to count every person in the United States for the purpose of apportioning seats in the U.S. House of Representatives.

Source: Census Bureau, Department of Commerce. Retrieved from http://www.census.gov.

Note: Census Bureau Homepage. The Census Bureau generates a huge stockpile of data about people, business and government.

But that's just a sliver of what's available from the Census Bureau. We can find demographic data that are much more detailed, as well as data about construction spending, retail trade, automobile registrations and home ownership. Dig deeper and you will find data about government employment, payrolls, debt levels, assets and budgets. Browse the navigation tabs on the Census Bureau website to get an idea of the data it collects and makes available. The bureau's American FactFinder provides an interactive tool that allows users to build customized tables from the decennial census and the American Community Survey, a data set with more demographic detail. The trade-off is that the ACS is based on a sample of the population and is not as statistically reliable as the decennial census.

The Bureau of Justice Statistics is a division of the U.S. Department of Justice and has published dozens of data sets about crime, justice and law enforcement (Bureau of Justice Statistics, n.d.). Criminologists, policy analysts and social scientists analyze these data to help identify trends in incarceration, hate crime, identity theft and human trafficking. The BJS regularly publishes reports that are based on its own analyses of the data, such as one in June 2013 that looked at indicators of school crime and safety in 2012 using the National Crime Victimization Survey (Snyder and Truman, 2013).

The Bureau of Transportation Statistics is part of the U.S. Department of Transportation and compiles data sets about air, highway, rail and waterway travel. It even has data about Canadian and Mexican border crossings and oil and gas pipelines. Commercial

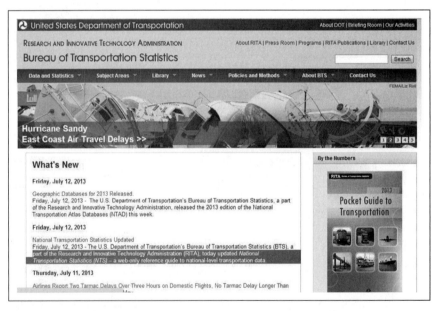

Source: Bureau of Transportation Statistics, Department of Transportation. Retrieved from http://www.rita.dot.gov/bts/.

Note: Bureau of Transportation Statistics website.

airport operators, journalists and airlines use BTS data to evaluate the cost of flying, on-time performance and general airport activity.

BTS's own researchers and others have used the data to create reports about drunken driving, container port activity and the impact of the 9/11 attacks on U.S. travel (Bureau of Transportation Statistics, n.d.).

For economic and employment statistics, the U.S. Department of Labor's Bureau of Labor Statistics is one of the best resources. BLS collects authoritative data about employment, the labor force, compensation, mass layoffs and inflation (through the Consumer Price Index and other indexes). In fact, the BLS data are the source of the government's official numbers for unemployment and inflation. Economists and economic development professionals use these data on the job. The best way to find the data is to navigate by either subject area or database name.

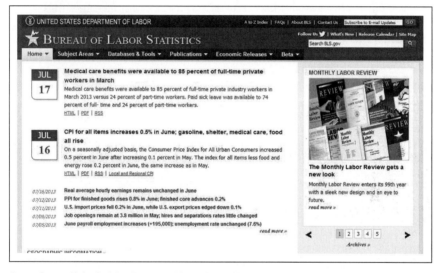

Source: Bureau of Labor Statistics, Department of Labor. Retrieved from http://www.bls.gov/home.htm.

Note: Bureau of Labor Statistics website.

Data about early childhood, primary, secondary, higher and adult education can be found on the National Center for Education Statistics site, run by the U.S. Department of Education. The center is a trove of data about costs, enrollment and crime at universities and other higher education institutions. It also provides data about student to teacher ratios at public schools. Recent reports using the center's data include looks at private and

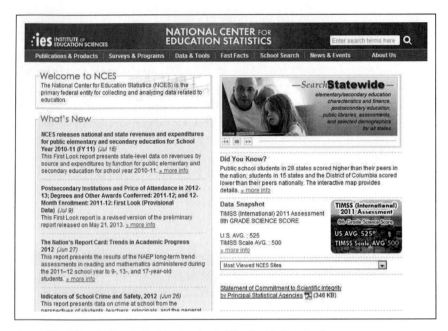

Source: National Center for Education Statistics, Department of Education, http://ies.ed.gov/.

Note: National Center for Education Statistics website.

public schools, and the most popular majors for bachelor's degrees (National Center for Education Statistics, n.d.).

AGENCY SITES

It's smart to become familiar with how agencies store data on their own sites, because only some data are hosted on or linked to data portals. This is where the hunt for data can get challenging because agencies sometimes scatter data around. Use website navigation tabs to look for words like Data, Open Data, Transparency and Statistics.

The Federal Deposit Insurance Corporation, for example, links to its data through its Industry Analysis navigation tab, then Bank Data & Statistics. The data include the Summary of Deposits, which has data about the amount of deposits taken in at each bank branch location. Marketing analysts and regulators use the data to examine the level of competition within banking markets.

See if the agency has its own data portal or page by typing the following in your browser: www.agencyname.gov/data. For example, entering "www.epa.gov/data" takes you to the EPA's Data Finder page.

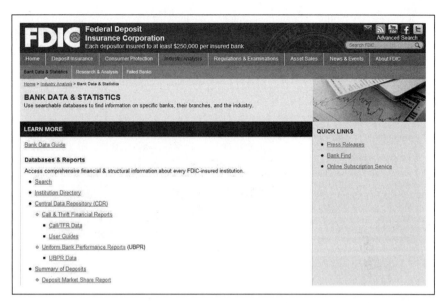

Source: Federal Deposit Insurance Corporation. Retrieved from https://www.fdic.gov/bank/statistical/index.html.

Note: Federal Deposit Insurance Corporation data about banks.

Source: Environmental Protection Agency. Retrieved from http://www.epa.gov/data/.

Note: Environmental Protection Agency data page. Try to find agency data pages by typing "/data" after the agency's main URL.

Or you can try typing data.agencyname.gov. To look for the Missouri state open data portal, you would type "data.mo.gov".

Source: Retrieved from Data.mo.gov.

Note: State of Missouri data portal. Try to find data portals by typing "data" instead of "www" in a URL.

NONGOVERNMENTAL RESOURCES

Data from government agencies are used widely because they are considered to be an authoritative record. In addition, government data (at least in the United States) are considered to be free of licensing rules that restrict distribution and use. For journalists, official documents and data provide an additional benefit: protection against libel suits. The fair report privilege provides a shield to journalists who base their news accounts on fair and accurate use of official sources.

However, nongovernmental organizations (or NGOs) also offer online data that we can use for our analyses. The Right to Know Network, which we visited in Chapter 2, posts several databases from the EPA. The data are from the EPA, but are distributed by the Center for Effective Government through the RTKNet site. Aside from promoting government transparency, the center advocates for progressive revenues (Center for Effective Government, 2013) or higher tax rates for people with higher incomes (and vice versa). On the other side of the political spectrum, Missouri's Show-Me Institute posts salary data for public employees that site visitors can download into an ASCII text file. The institute is a nonprofit organization that promotes free market and libertarian solutions to social and governmental problems. The institute gets its payroll data from the State Department of Administration.

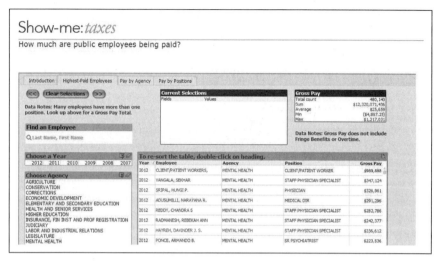

Source: Show-Me Institute. Retrieved from http://www.showmeliving.org/payroll.

Note: Missouri state data posted on the nongovernmental Show-Me Institute's website.

Before using data from a nongovernmental source, ask,

- How did the NGO obtain the data?
- What did the NGO do to process or change the data?
- What interest does the NGO have in making the data available?
- Can you get the data directly from the official government source instead?

Some NGO sites collect data that are not from governmental sources. The Roper Center at the University of Connecticut and the Gallup Company both offer access to archives with public opinion polling data. The Inter-university Consortium for Political and Social Research at the University of Michigan archives data from social science researchers. If your college or university is a member of the consortium, you'll be able to download the data, assuming your computer is connected to your institution's network (Inter-university Consortium for Political and Social Research, n.d.).

DATA SEARCH TRICKS

Just as we used Google Advanced Search to uncover clues about data, we can use it to find data files that we can download. The trick is to think of words that appear on webpages with downloadable data and plug those into our search form. Let's revisit the EPA's data page at http://www.epa.gov/data for some ideas. We see that "downloadable" and "data" appear multiple times, which leads us to believe those terms will work well for our search. Go ahead and try "downloadable data site .gov" to look for pages with "downloadable" and "data" on websites that have .gov extensions. Your results list should have a mix of federal, state and local websites. Of course, you could try to narrow your search further: for example, if you wanted to find only Excel files add "filetype:xls". Try different search terms, such as "download data," and see what happens.

DON'T FORGET THE ROAD MAP

When downloading data from a government website, make sure you also download a copy of any documentation. The **data documentation**, often stored as a Word, PDF or other document file, usually is essential in helping understand what's in the data file. There's no standard name for the documentation, so it might be called record layout, file layout, data dictionary or something entirely different. If you can't download the documentation, try to get a copy of it from someone at the agency, using contact information that's on the website.

Whatever the name, the documentation usually provides some key pieces of information about the data set:

- Table names, along with record counts for each table.
- Column or field names in each table, along with a field description, type of field (character, number, date, etc.) and width.
- Codes and their meanings. Data are often stored in codes, so the documentation should explain these.

For example, the Federal Aviation Administration routinely collects data about licensed pilots and releases some of these data in the Airman Directory Releasable File. On the same webpage where the FAA releases the data in two different text file formats, it also provides documentation for each (Federal Aviation Administration, n.d.). This example from the nine-page documentation for the **CSV** (comma-separated value, or delimited text) file says we have a table called Pilot Basic, which has 13 columns or fields, starting with UNIQUE ID and ending with MEDICAL EXPIRE DATE. All of the fields are formatted as A, or alphanumeric. (**Alphanumeric** data use characters to represent numbers and text.) The lengths tell us how many characters can be stored in each column. The remarks provide information about codes used (see the remarks for MEDICAL CLASS) and that the dates are stored in the MEDICAL DATE and MEDICAL EXPIRE DATE columns as MMYYYY (or month, month, year, year, year, year).

FIELD NAME	FORMAT	LENGTH	REMARKS
Pilot Basic record file			
UNIQUE ID	A	8	1st position = 'A' or 'C' followed by a 7-digit number
FIRST & MIDDLE NAME	A	30	
LAST NAME & SUFFIX	A	30	
STREET 1	A	33	
STREET 2	A	33	
CITY	A	17	
STATE	A	2	Blank if foreign address
ZIP CODE	A	10	
COUNTRY-NAME	A	18	
REGION	A	2	
MEDICAL CLASS	A	1	1=First 2=Second 3=Third (Certificate Type "P" only)
MEDICAL DATE	A	6	MMYYYY (Certificate Type "P" only)
MEDICAL EXPIRE DATE	A	6	MMYYYY (Certificate Type "P" only)

Source: Airmen Certification Database. (n.d.). FAA: Home. Retrieved July 22, 2013, from http://www.faa.gov/licenses_certificates/airmen_certification/releasable_airmen_download/

Note: File documentation for the Federal Aviation Administration's airmen database.

DOWNLOADING, UNZIPPING AND INSPECTING DATA FILES

In the final part of this chapter, we are going to download, unzip and inspect a delimited text file. We'll work with fuel economy data from the U.S. Department of Energy kept at http://www.fueleconomy.gov/feg/download.shtml. Under Find and Compare Cars Data, download the CSV file to a location on your computer where you can easily retrieve it. Then click on the Documentation link, which is our guide to understanding the contents of each column. (Make sure you record the details about the data in your data notebook. Do this for all of the data you download.)

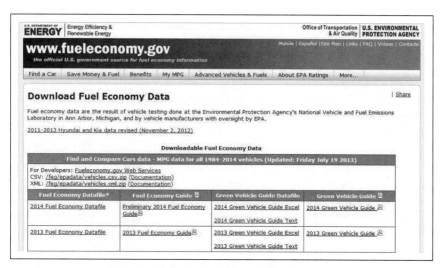

Source: Department of Energy. Retrieved from http://www.fueleconomy.gov/feg/download.shtml.

Note: Federal government website for vehicle fuel economy data.

Find the file using Windows Explorer (or Finder if you are using a Mac). Right-click on the file and pick Extract All . . . to launch the Windows unzipping utility. Change the destination of the extracted files if you wish and then click Extract. You now have a folder called vehicles.csv that contains a file of the same name. The compressed files usually are called **zip files** and have a .zip extension.

Source: Department of Energy.

Note: Comma-separated values file containing data about vehicle fuel efficiency. Windows computers usually display CSV files as Excel files.

Windows identifies the file as a Microsoft Excel Comma Separated Values File. Because the .csv file extension is associated with Excel, you can double-click on the file to open it. Use Ctrl-End to navigate to the end of the file; you'll see it has 33,847 rows. Close the file now and don't save any changes, if prompted.

Vehicles.csv is a text—not an Excel—file, so we can view it in a text editor program. On Windows, we'll use Notepad++, which is a free and open-source program that we can download from http://notepad-plus-plus.org/. Notepad++ has many more features than the stock Notepad that comes with Windows; it can open larger files than Notepad can, also. (Mac users, install TextWrangler, which is a free program available at http://www .barebones.com/products/textwrangler/.)

Open vehicles.csv with your text editor and you should see something like this:

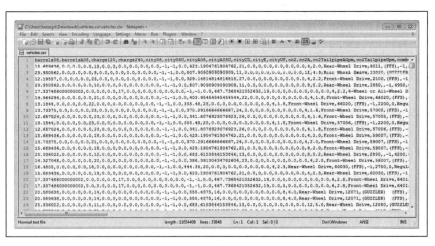

Source: Department of Energy.

Note: Comma-separated values in a text editor. Note the commas, which are used for column delimiters, and the compressed data.

It looks like a mess, as if someone took our data and squished them together. Actually, this is how comma-delimited text files are supposed to look. The first line contains the labels for our columns. Each comma denotes a column break to Excel and other programs. The first line of data starts on the second line. Use Ctrl-End to navigate to the end of the Notepad++ file and you'll see we have 33,847 rows—the same number we did when we opened it in Excel.

Now, let's download, unzip and inspect some tab-delimited data that are produced by the Food and Drug Administration for its Total Diet Study, which is supposed to monitor the levels of contaminants in food. The Total Diet Study was started in 1961 as a program for detecting radiation. Since then, it has expanded to look for the presence of pesticides and industrial chemicals in food (Food and Drug Administration, n.d.). Navigate to the analytical results page at http://www.fda.gov/ForConsumers/ConsumerUpdates/ucm184293.htm and download the O 2008 file under the Elements heading. Find the file named FY 08 O results only.zip and unzip it. You now have a text file called FY 08 O results only.txt. Excel does not recognize the .txt extension as a native file, so we can't just click on it to open it. Instead, open it using your text editor. The file should look something like this:

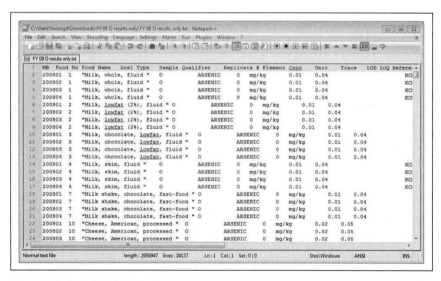

Source: Food and Drug Administration.

Note: At first glance, no delimiters are in this delimited-data file.

Again, because this is a delimited text file, it looks like a mess—with squished-together data. We notice that the first row contains the column headers. The data themselves start in the second row. Also, some of the data have double quotation marks. These are called **text qualifiers** and are sometimes used in delimited text data to denote text that should be kept intact inside a column. Single quotation marks also can be used as text qualifiers.

But where are the delimiters—the tabs? Tabs are considered ASCII characters, but they are hidden, so we normally don't see them. In Notepad++, we can make them appear by going to View I Show Symbol in the menu, then selecting Show All Characters.

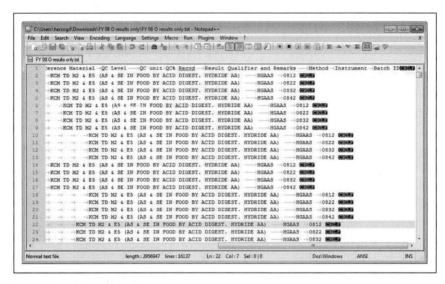

Source: Food and Drug Administration.

Note: Tab characters used as delimiters, no longer hidden.

Aha! Now we can see reddish arrows. Those are the tabs that serve as the column delimiters. We also see some periods, which represent spaces. Let's now scroll over to the right side of the file and we can see two black blocks with white text. They say CR and LF and mean carriage return and line feed. These are hidden ASCII characters that are used to denote an end of the data record.

Source: Microsoft Excel 2013 for Windows.

Note: Opening files in Excel

One last check: Let's use Ctrl-End to see how many lines of data we have. We should see 16,136, including header row. Close the text file now.

Time to open the file in Excel. Start Excel and then Open Other Workbooks in the pane on the left. Select Computer and then use the Browse button to the right to look for the extracted text file.

We won't see any files because Excel is looking only for native Excel files. Change the File type option at the bottom right to All Files and the text file appears. Open it, and Excel launches a text import wizard that walks us through the process of opening the file.

In Step 1, we need to tell Excel what kind of text file—delimited or fixed-width—we're importing. Excel has correctly guessed delimited. (Excel sometimes gets this wrong, so make sure to check this.) Our data have headers in the first row, so we need check the box that says My data has headers and start the import at Row 1 to capture these data.

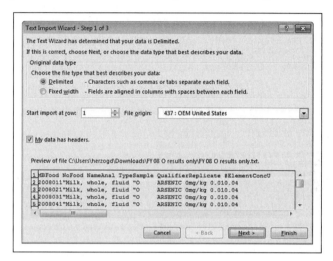

Source: Microsoft Excel 2013 for Windows.

Note: Step 1 in the Excel text import wizard.

In the next step, we need to specify the delimiter character, so make sure the box for Tab is checked. (If we need to specify a character other than any of those listed, just check the Other box and enter the character in the box next to it.) At this step, we also need to tell the wizard that we're using double quotation marks as text qualifiers.

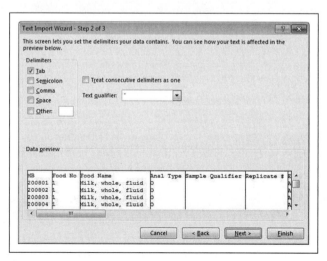

Source: Microsoft Excel 2013 for Windows.

Note: Step 2 in the Excel text import wizard.

Last, we need to tell Excel what data types to apply to each column. The default often is General, which means Excel takes a look at the contents of each column and makes an educated guess about the format. This can be a problem because we might have a column that includes zip codes, some of which have leading zeros. Take 02818 in East Greenwich, Rhode Island, for example. If Excel imports this as general, it will treat it as a number and lop off the leading zero, leaving a zip code of 2818. Fortunately, we have a simple workaround: making the column text. We really should make all of the columns text to avoid any import flubs that may delete data. We can always change the format of the column in Excel later.

We can change the formats for all of the columns quickly by highlighting the first column, then scrolling to the final column and selecting it with Ctrl-click. Now that all of the columns are highlighted, select Text as the column data format.

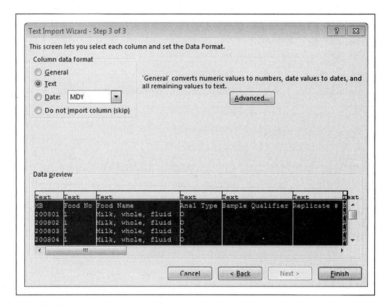

Source: Microsoft Excel 2013 for Windows.

Note: Step 3 in the Excel text import wizard.

Now click Finish, and Excel does the rest of the work. Depending on your software settings, Excel displays green flags, which are just alerts saying data that look like numbers have been formatted as text.

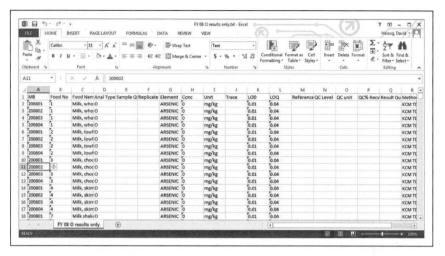

Source: Food and Drug Administration.

Note: Text file successfully imported in Excel.

We haven't yet saved this as an Excel file, so let's do that by clicking on the File tab, then selecting Save As. Browse to a location where you are storing your files, and select Excel Workbook (*.xlsx) as the file type. That does it!

In this chapter we've covered a lot of ground, starting with identifying useful data on the Internet. We also learned how to download, unzip and inspect ASCII files in a text editor.

In the next chapter, we'll turn our attention to how we can learn about all of the data that government agencies keep offline and how we can obtain them informally or formally through open-records requests.

ON YOUR OWN

Use Google Advanced Search to find data that your state or local government keeps online. Give three examples of data that you found and a brief summary of each example. Also, provide the search syntax you used to uncover these data.

Find the data portal for your state or local government. How did you find it? Provide summaries of three data sets that are on the portal.

CHAPTER 4   IDENTIFYING AND REQUESTING OFFLINE DATA

As we saw in the previous chapter, government agencies are posting a growing number of data sets on the Internet. However, most governmental data sets are held offline for a variety of reasons, such as lack of financial or human resources, political sensitivity and the perception that the public might not be interested in the data. Finding online data can be tough, but it can be even more challenging to identify and successfully obtain databases that government agencies store offline. In this chapter we will learn some approaches for further developing a data state of mind to become more aware of these offline data sets. We'll also learn how to use federal and state open-records laws to make formal requests for these databases, which are public information. Knowing the name of the database and how it's kept is key to making a successful request using the federal Freedom of Information Act or similar state laws.

In Chapter 2, we learned that some government agencies collect and use data because they're required to by law or because it helps them meet their strategic goals. We learned that we can uncover clues about databases by looking for data entry with handheld computers or with paper and electronic forms and in statistical reports. In Chapter 3, we learned about data documentation. We can use all of these clues to help uncover offline databases.

OTHER CLUES FOR OFFLINE DATA

Some tools are particularly well suited for helping identify offline data. These are resources such as records retention schedules, audit reports, federal agency major information system listings and nongovernmental organization sites.

Records retention schedules provide details about records held by state and local government agencies, and guidelines about how long those agencies need to keep the records. Each state issues its own records retention schedules for state records, and sometimes issues a separate schedule for local records. Unfortunately, there is little uniformity from one state to another about what's in the schedules and how to access them. The Georgia Secretary of State provides a lookup form for its schedule. The Florida Department of State offers the information in PDF, Word or Excel format. The Utah Department of Administrative Services offers the information as webpages that you need to click through until you've found what you're after. The example below shows that Utah state agencies are supposed to keep records about the sale of state-owned real estate for six years. The entry fails to mention whether any of the information is available as data, but at least we know there's a possibility.

REAL PROPERTY SALE FILES (ITEM 14-3)

Records which document the transfer of state owned real estate to non-state ownership, whether by transfer, trade, sale, or donation.

RETENTION

Record copy: Permanent. Retain by agency for 6 years after a deed of sale is recorded and then transfer to State Archives with authority to weed.

Duplicate copies: Retain until administrative need ends and then destroy.

SUGGESTED PRIMARY DESIGNATION

Public.

(Approved 07/90)

Source: Utah Department of Administrative Services. Retrieved from http://archives.utah.gov/recordsmanagement/grs/stgrs-14.html.

Note: Entry from Utah's records retention schedule.

Most records retention schedules do not distinguish whether a record is kept in a database or on paper. The schedules for Texas, Delaware, Ohio and New York State are some of the exceptions, in that they mention computer files.

Find records retention schedules by searching or by going to the Council of State Archivists website, which has links for state (http://www.statearchivists.org/arc/states/res_sch_genlst.htm) and local records (http://www.statearchivists.org/arc/states/res_sch_genlloc.htm) schedules.

Audit reports generated by state or federal authorities examine the operations of government. The Government Accountability Office, which is the investigative arm of Congress, monitors the performance of agencies and issues in-depth reports with results and recommendations for improvement. The reports can easily run dozens of pages, but you can get to the meat quickly by reading, in the full PDF report, the Summary of Findings or What GAO Found section, as well as the Scope and Methodology. If a GAO auditor reviewed any databases for the report, he or she will list those in the Scope and Methodology. In the states, auditors who are elected in statewide elections conduct audits and generate similar reports we can use for getting clues about data.

Federal inspectors' general reports might also be helpful. Inspectors' general offices are independent units within federal agencies and are supposed to investigate possible fraud, waste and other wrongdoing. Look for references to databases in these reports, too.

For example, this audit report from the U.S. Department of Agriculture examines the Farm Assistance Program payments by the Farm Service Agency in the federal government's 2012 fiscal year. The inspector general says the FSA failed to adequately document payments. In the Scope and Methodology section of the report, the inspector general noted that it used a sample of program payment data for its audit (Department of Agriculture, 2013). So we know that there's a database of payments that we could request.

Scope and Methodology

We obtained the universe of payments from FSA and statistically selected 80 payments made from October 1, 2011, through September 30, 2012.[12] FSA provided four data extracts that included program payments for all of fiscal year 2012, totaling $759 million. FSA made the payments through 11 programs.[13]

Source: Fiscal Year 2012 Farm Service Agency Farm Assistance Program Payments. (n.d.). U.S. Dept. of Agriculture. Retrieved July 24, 2013, from www.usda.gov/oig/webdocs/03401-0002-11.pdf.

Note: Methodology from federal inspector general report. The methodology shows that the inspector general obtained four data extracts for its examination.

Governmental and nongovernmental websites have a lot to say about data that are kept offline by agencies. Under the Electronic Freedom of Information Act Amendments (**E-FOIA**) of 1996, federal agencies are supposed to provide an index and description of their major information system webpages (Department of Justice, 1996).

The Act, signed into law by President Bill Clinton, directed federal agencies to create electronic reading rooms on their websites where the agencies could post documents and data requested repeatedly under FOIA. The electronic reading rooms are supposed to be the spot where we can find the lists of major information systems as well.

Some agencies have been better than others at disclosing details about their major information systems.

In fact, in 2007 most federal agencies were failing to comply with the law's requirement to post indexes and descriptions of their major information systems, according to a study by the National Security Archive at The George Washington University. As of that year, roughly one out of every three agencies had posted detailed information:

Contrary to Congress's intent to make agency record-keeping more transparent, the manner in which agencies present record indexes and guides varies widely and is more confusing than helpful for requesters. Many agencies have not attempted to describe their record holdings in a systematic and comprehensive way. The indexes and major information system descriptions that are available vary widely in format and usability. . . .

Unfortunately, this congressional mandate has failed, at least with respect to providing the public insight into agency record-keeping and publicly available information. (National Security Archive, 2007)

More recently, some federal agencies, such as the Drug Enforcement Administration, began removing the major information system listings on their own sites and referring site visitors to the Federal IT Dashboard at https://itdashboard.gov/ (Drug Enforcement Administration, n.d.a).

Some other agencies, such as the U.S. Postal Service and the U.S. Marshals Service, continue to have their own listings. For instance, the Marshals Service lists the Warrant Information System as one of its dozen databases that it uses (Marshals Service, n.d.a.).

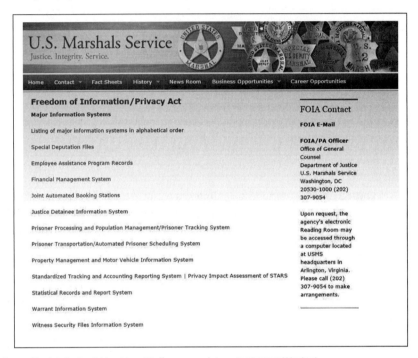

Source: Marshals Service. Retrieved from http://www.usmarshals.gov/readingroom/titles.html.

Note: Marshals Service major information systems.

A new initiative by the Obama administration could plug some of these holes. Under the White House's 2013 Open Data Policy, federal agencies are supposed to create data inventories and post public versions of them (Sinai and Van Dyck, 2013). If implemented properly, these inventories could help to identify the offline databases.

Nongovernmental websites can also tell you about what data these agencies have. The National Institute for Computer-Assisted Reporting Database Library, which is run by the Missouri School of Journalism and Investigative Reporters and Editors, lists more than 40 data sets from the federal government. Only journalists who are members of IRE may purchase the data, but anyone can scout for details about databases at the site. As an example, the database library (which the author has helped direct) provides data about federal contracts. Anyone can see detailed information about this database, noting that it is produced by the U.S. General Services Administration.

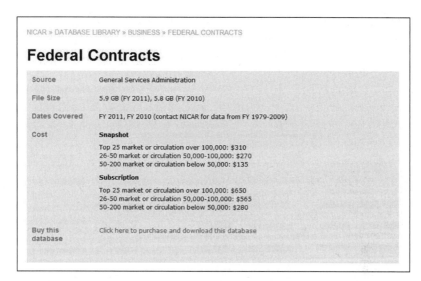

Source: National Institute for Computer-Assisted Reporting. Retrieved from http://www.ire.org/nicar/database-library/databases/federal-contracts/.

Note: NICAR Database Library entry for federal contracts data available to journalists.

Then there are sites aimed at informing the public about data held by state and local agencies. OpenMissouri (launched by the author in 2011) provides details about some 250 databases held by state agencies. This example from the state Department of Agriculture provides details about an egg license database that is exportable to an Excel spreadsheet (OpenMissouri.org, n.d.).

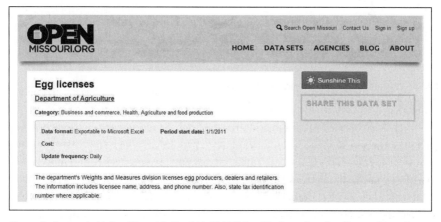

Source: Egg licenses. (n.d.). Open Missouri. Retrieved July 25, 2013, from http://openmissouri.org/data_sets/51-egg-licenses

Note: OpenMissouri entry for egg license data from the Missouri Department of Agriculture.

Another nongovernmental source that can be tapped to find information about offline data in all 50 states is the State Agency Databases wiki of the American Library Association's Government Documents Roundtable (http://wikis.ala.org/godort/index.php/State_Agency_Databases). Volunteer librarians who are specialists in government documents and data have compiled the information since 2007 by scouring state agency websites for searchable online databases. Often, these sites lack data that we can download. But we do know that there are databases behind these search forms that we can request.

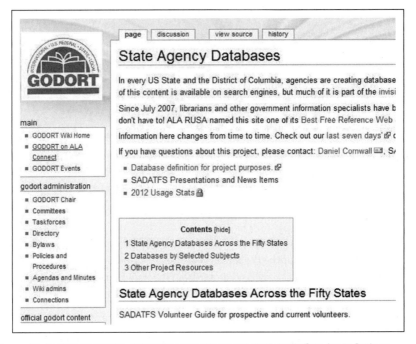

Source: American Library Association. Retrieved from http://wikis.ala.org/godort/index.php/State_Agency_Databases.

Note: State Agency Databases wiki. Volunteers from the American Library Association attempt to track state agency databases on this wiki.

Let's visit the page for Colorado and look for the Cold Case Database, listed under Public Safety (https://www.colorado.gov/apps/coldcase/index.html).

By clicking on the Search tab and then the Click for more search options box, we can see that users can search a number of ways: first, last or alias name, case type, case status, gender, age, year, race, eyes, hair, city, county, status, agency and more. It's a pretty safe guess that because the information is broken down that way on the search form that there's a data table (or tables) with those columns of data. So we could request that table from the Colorado Bureau of Investigation, which is the agency that keeps the data.

Source: Colorado Bureau of Investigation. Retrieved from https://www.colorado.gov/apps/coldcase/index.html.

Note: State of Colorado cold case database search.

FIND THE DATA NERD

After you've identified an offline database, you may need to do some more research before you can request and obtain it. The agency employees who create or maintain the data can be helpful because they are the ones who are most familiar with the system used for storing and retrieving the data. Sometimes you can find technical contact information on the government websites. Other times, you might need to call or email the agency to find the right contact person. In some government agencies, public affairs officers may try to prevent you from talking directly to the employees most familiar with the data. That's unfortunate, because public affairs officers are not as familiar with the data and can make the process more complex than it has to be. As a negotiating tactic, you can always ask to speak to the data specialist directly, in the interests of making things easier for everyone. That way the burden will be lessened for the public affairs officer.

When you gather information about the offline database, you may need to address a range of technical issues about how the data are stored, processed and formatted. These discussions can get pretty involved, but they usually touch on three common areas: the physical device on which the data are stored, the database software used to process and manipulate the data and the format in which the file is stored.

Some governments use **mainframe** computers for their data processing. Mainframes are large, powerful machines that can run multiple processes and have been around since the 1960s. Though mainframes are costly and sometimes seen as outmoded, they still remain popular in some businesses (Lohr, 2012). Other government agencies often employ computer servers to run their database programs. Computer **servers** are less expensive than mainframes, but they also are unable to process the same amounts of data. Many times a computer server is dedicated to one task. Desktop computers—like Windows PCs and Macs—are the least powerful of the bunch and usually do not host database programs. That said, government agency employees sometimes do create spreadsheets and databases that they then access on their own computers.

Another consideration is the computer software that's used to store and manipulate the data. Sometimes that will be a spreadsheet program, such as Excel. However, it's more likely that an agency uses a database manager. Database managers are often relational—they allow users to relate multiple tables to each other. Government agencies usually run commercial database software, such as IBM's DB2, Oracle, Sybase, Microsoft SQL Server or Microsoft Access. All of those programs run on servers or mainframes, with the exception of Access, which is a Windows desktop program. Open-source database manager programs, such as MySQL or PostgreSQL, are less common in government agencies.

Unfortunately, all of these database programs store the data in their own formats, which are incompatible with each other. If agencies are unable to produce Excel files, they should be able to create ASCII text (delimited or fixed-width), because that is the format common to all computers.

REQUESTING THE DATA

After you know the name of the database and something about how the agency can provide it to you, you'll need to request it. You can make an informal request for the data just by asking for it by phone or in an email. Sometimes that works. Other times, you will need to make a formal request using the federal or a state open-records law.

If you want to get copies of offline data from a federal government agency, such as the DEA or EPA, you need to file a Freedom of Information Act request. If you want to get data from the state or any of the governmental entities within it, you would need to request those data using that state's open-records law. So, if you wanted data from your local police department or county sheriff's office, you would need to exercise your rights under your state's open-records law.

Both FOIA, enacted in 1966, and state open-records laws start from the premise that all information collected by the government for public purposes is open. Even though FOIA and all of the state laws differ on many details, they all define some key points: response time, acceptable responses, exemptions, data formats and costs. We'll look at how FOIA and one state law—the Missouri Sunshine Law—compare.

FOIA gives the federal agencies 20 working days to respond to requests, compared to 3 working days under the Missouri Sunshine Law. Federal agencies are required only to respond with an acknowledgement that they received a request, so requesters can wait a long time to get data. Some journalists have waited years to get files from the Federal Bureau of Investigation, for example. In Missouri, agencies are supposed to provide the data or deny the request, by providing legal reasons for doing so within the three working days. They are also allowed to take more time to fill the request, as long as they provide a legitimate reason.

All the laws provide exemptions that allow government agencies to hold data that are considered nonpublic. FOIA has nine standard exemptions—including one for law enforcement materials whose disclosure could reasonably be expected to disclose the identity of a confidential source. Another exemption blocks the release of documents that are properly classified as secret in the interest of national defense or foreign policy. The Missouri law has a number of exemptions, including some arrest records and calls to 911 dispatch centers. Both laws have big loopholes in that they allow for records to be excluded by other laws.

Another key consideration is how the laws treat requests for data. Most of the laws—including the Missouri Sunshine Law and FOIA—specifically state that electronic data are public, just as paper documents are. In addition, some laws specify what rights you have in terms of the data format desired. Under FOIA, federal agencies are supposed to provide data in the format that's requested if the agency is able to do so. Under the Missouri Sunshine Law, the format in which the data are stored is considered the public record. Agencies are not required to produce data in other formats, though the law encourages them to do so.

Public-records laws outline allowable costs. FOIA allows federal agencies to pass along copying and reviewing costs. The Missouri Sunshine Law allows agencies to charge copying and staff salary costs. In addition, agencies can pass along programming costs when they choose to create a new record by putting existing records into a different format. FOIA and the Sunshine Law allow agencies to waive costs if the information contained in the request is in the public interest, something that's part of most state laws. Some states even allow requesters to limit their fees to a certain dollar amount.

WRITING THE DATA REQUEST

A good open-records request letter is clear, concise and includes enough detail about what you are seeking. The letter should include

- The name and contact information for the person filling the request;
- Citation of the law under which the request is being made;
- The name of the database, as it's known inside the agency;
- The names of the data columns, if known;
- The time frame of the data;
- The format in which you'd like to receive the data (along with the medium);
- Request for the documentation;
- Request for written explanation, in case of denial;
- Fee waiver request or limitation; and
- Your contact information.

The Reporters Committee for Freedom of the Press has an online service called iFOIA that allows users to build customized federal or state request letters; https://www.ifoia .org/#!/.

Source: Reporters Committee for Freedom of the Press. Retrieved from https://www.ifoia.org/#!/.

Note: iFOIA from the Reporters Committee for Freedom of the Press.

FOIA IN ACTION

As a Washington correspondent for *The New York Times*, Ron Nixon uses data frequently in his reporting on federal agencies. (The following discussion is based on Nixon 2013.) Nixon has used data for stories about how elderly people have been killed or injured by dangerous bed rails in assisted-living and nursing homes, and how companies with federal contracts also do business in Iran, despite U.S. government sanctions.

Sometimes he can get what he needs from U.S. government websites or by making an informal request with someone who works for an agency. If those two avenues fail, Nixon says, he files FOIA requests for the data.

Nixon estimated that he files two or three FOIA requests a month, trying to obtain data for stories that he has on his to-do list. Getting data pursuant to a FOIA request can take a while, so Nixon says he tries to give himself plenty of time.

When he requests data, Nixon says he tries to be as specific as possible; he avoids making requests for everything in the database because FOIA officers in agencies usually kick back those requests. "They always want you to narrow it down," Nixon says. "If you know what you're looking for, it helps."

Nixon recommends that requesters "do a lot of leg work" before filing requests. For instance, Nixon sometimes bases his requests on the information that's collected on federal forms. Sometimes he looks at online federal agency FOIA logs to see what data others have already requested. If someone has already requested and received data, the agency should be able to easily provide a copy of those data.

When making FOIA requests, Nixon says to remember that fulfilling them is not a priority for federal agencies. Agencies do not have enough FOIA staff to do the job well. Remember that the FOIA staff members are overwhelmed, he says, and try to be as nice as possible to them when making or following up on requests.

NEGOTIATING THROUGH OBSTACLES

In real life, getting the data you need can be tough: government agencies can put up many obstacles, some of them legitimate and others not. Some of the common obstacles are privacy issues, cost and ability to produce the data.

Often, government agencies will tell you that they're unable to produce the data because the data are private, which may very well be true. However, under FOIA and the state open-records laws, the agencies are supposed to specify the section of the law that makes these data private. Just because someone thinks data are (or should be) private, doesn't mean that they truly are under the law. Ask agencies to cite the law in writing so you have a copy of the agency's legal reasoning on the record.

If some of the data truly are private, you can probably get the public portion of the data. That's because under FOIA and the state open-records laws, agencies are supposed to disclose what's public. For example, federal law prohibits the unauthorized disclosure of Social Security numbers. If you want to get a database of city employees that includes Social Security numbers, city hall is supposed to redact those private data and give you the rest.

An alphabet soup's list of federal privacy laws—FERPA, HIPAA and DPPA—could bar disclosure of some data stored in government databases.

FERPA is the **Family Educational Rights and Privacy Act**, and ensures the privacy of student educational records. Students have control of these records when they turn 18 or attend a school after high school. Before that, parents have control of the records.

Regulations drafted under FERPA allow school officials with a legitimate educational interest to have access to these records (Department of Education, n.d.). FERPA can become a stumbling block when people seek data from public schools or universities. Public colleges have denied requests for campus arrest records based on FERPA. The Student Press Law Center, which provides assistance to scholastic and university journalists, says FERPA ranks among the most common complaints that it receives and provides a PDF guide to help requesters work through denials (Gregory, 2013).

HIPAA is the **Health Insurance Portability and Accountability Act** of 1996, which protects individually identifiable health information (Department of Health and Human Services, n.d.). No one would argue that our personal medical data should be released without our consent.

DPPA, or the **Drivers Privacy Protection Act**, passed in 1994 after a number of high-profile incidents in which stalkers were able to get home address information from state motor vehicle departments. DPPA restricts states from releasing the personal data contained in a person's driving record (epic.org, n.d.). The law, however, does allow the data to be provided for a number of purposes, including insurance, motor vehicle recalls and court proceedings.

Costs can also become an obstacle. Agencies will sometimes say that providing the data will cost a lot of money. Ask for a price quote in writing, with a breakdown of costs that includes whatever is allowed under the law: copying, research, programming and so on. Even if the cost of the data is reasonable under the law, it still may be more than you can pay. Remember, you can always ask for a fee waiver in your request. Make sure that you research the conditions for the waiver and state how your request meets these conditions.

Another real world obstacle is difficulty in getting the data in a format that you can use. In Missouri, state agencies only must produce data in their original format. So, if the state department of higher education has a particular database that's stored as an Oracle file, it doesn't have to produce an Excel or ASCII file. In other cases, an agency may claim that it lacks the expertise to produce the data in a format that you can use. Or the agency might have outsourced its information technology operations to a third-party vendor, making it difficult to figure out exactly how the vendor could output the data for you. Fortunately, most state laws say that government agencies cannot avoid their obligations under open-records laws by outsourcing their database operations to private vendors.

GETTING HELP

Negotiating for information (whether data or documents) from public agencies truly is an art, one that requires more knowledge and nuance than this chapter can provide. If you want more in-depth guidance, check out *The Art of Access* by David Cuillier and Charles N. Davis (2011). It's a great how-to guide that's written for journalism students and working journalists, but the lessons can be applied by people in any field.

Another great resource is the Open Government Guide from the Reporters Committee for Freedom of the Press, which is a nonprofit organization that assists journalists.

The OGG provides detailed information about FOIA, federal privacy and state open-records laws. The guide includes specific information about how the laws treat data.

In some states, dedicated agencies can sometimes assist in data requests. In Connecticut anyone who's denied a request for data or other records under the state Freedom of Information Act can appeal that decision to the Freedom of Information Commission. The FOI Commission holds hearings about the complaints and decides whether the agencies have violated the law. If the agency has violated the law, the commission may order the agency to produce the data (Connecticut Office of Governmental Accountability, n.d.).

In Texas, the attorney general's office gets involved in some data requests. When an agency denies information, the agency is supposed to ask for a decision from the AG's office. Both the requester and the agency denying the information are then allowed to provide input to the AG's office (Attorney General of Texas: Greg Abbott, n.d.).

In addition to these official government agencies, you can get help from nongovernmental organizations. A good starting point for identifying such groups in your state is the National Freedom of Information Coalition, which is based at the University of Missouri. The NFOIC (www.nfoic.org) represents the interests of state-level open government groups and, on its website, provides links to them. So, if someone in Florida is looking for help with challenges getting data from a state or local agency, he or she can go to the NFOIC site, follow a link to the Florida First Amendment Foundation and seek help from that organization.

Source: National Freedom of Information Coalition. Retrieved from www.nfoic.org.

Note: National Freedom of Information Coalition website. The NFOIC represents the interests of state-level open government groups.

As we've seen, it can be tough to identify and obtain data that are held offline, as government agencies do not readily inform us about the data they keep. Fortunately, we can use the clues—such as records retention schedules and search forms—to uncover databases. Then, we can ask for the data informally, or make a formal open-records request.

Our next step in working with the data is testing them, so we know their flaws and limits. Only after that can we analyze and visualize them.

ON YOUR OWN

Find your state's open-records law. Cite it and write a few paragraphs describing the process for requesting data. Include details about any appeals or possible intervention by government officials in other agencies.

Identify three possible offline databases in your state by using the American Library Association's State Agency Databases wiki. Cite the URLs and write a summary of what columns of data the databases might contain.

Identify your state or local open-government group using the NFOIC membership list. Record the URL for the group's website and contact information. Note whether the group provides any assistance to the public.

Find a federal GAO or state audit report that mentions a database. Cite the report and write a brief summary of the database and how the auditors used it.

Find an instance in which FERPA privacy concerns by a public agency have resulted in student journalists being denied data or other information. Summarize the details. Do you believe this denial was legitimate? Why or why not?

Write a mock open-records request letter asking for public employee data from your city for the past three years. Request the data as an Excel file, to be provided via email.

Find your state in the Reporters Committee for Freedom of the Press Open Government Guide. How does your state's law treat data? Does the law say computerized data are public records? What does the law say in terms of your rights to request data in a particular format? Cite the law and write a summary.

EVALUATING AND CLEANING DATA

CHAPTER 5 **DATA DIRT IS EVERYWHERE**

W hen we get a data file—by downloading it or through a public records request—it's tempting to want to start analyzing it right away.

Many students and even professionals would like to dive in by starting to run calculations to generate some results. But, at this point, we need to pause and take time to understand our data better. What are the data's strengths? What are their weaknesses? Is anything missing? How important are those missing data? Can we use the data to accurately answer any questions that we might have? Do we need to get other data that might better answer our questions?

All of these questions deal with academic and professional ethics—particularly our responsibility to represent the world as truthfully as we can. As analysts, we have a duty to know our data inside and out. We need to have an intimate understanding of their shortcomings. We owe the consumers of our data analysis—whether that's other researchers, business clients or the public—the most accurate reading of our data that we can possibly deliver. This is even more crucial in an era when pretty much anyone can easily contribute and consume data on the Internet, and interact with each other. In our networked world, sharing information is almost a trivial act, albeit one that can magnify error tremendously. If we are careful and ethical, we can offer thoughtful analysis.

Blindly trusting that government agencies and others will collect and report data accurately is a neglect of duty on our part. Veteran data users will tell you that government data files run the gamut from slightly messy to so flawed that the data are unusable.

Why? Aren't government agencies and other producers of data supposed to get it right? The reality is that government agencies often have poor data quality control, if they have any at all.

Here's an example from California, where the state Department of Education offers student-discipline data for schools for download on its website (California Department of Education, n.d.b). California, and in fact all states, must disclose data about discipline under the No Child Left Behind Act of 2001. This law was championed by President George W. Bush as a tool for improving the academic performance of disadvantaged children.

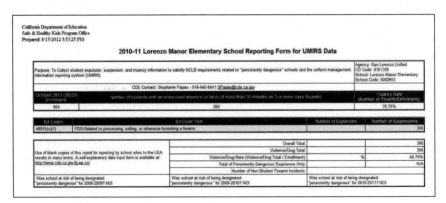

Source: California Department of Education. Retrieved from http://dq.cde.ca.gov/dataquest/.

Note: California search tool for student public school performance data.

Under the law, local school districts are supposed to report detailed data about student performance, including discipline, to state educational authorities. In California, one elementary school, with 654 students, reported it had suspended students 306 times for bringing guns to school in the 2010–2011 school year. That reported number was clearly an outlier. In each of the five previous school years for which there are data the school never reported more than 131 suspensions for all reasons, and not just firearms incidents (California Department of Education, n.d.a).

Source: Lorenzo Manor Elementary School - Suspension & Expulsion Information. (n.d.). DataQuest CA Dept. of Education. Retrieved June 13, 2013, from http://dq.cde.ca.gov/dataquest/Expulsion/ExpReports/SchoolExpRe.aspx?cYear=2010-11&cCho ice=ExpInfo3&cDistrict=0161309--San%20Lorenzo%20Unified&cCounty=01,ALAMEDA&cNumber=6002653&cName=LORE NZO%20MANOR%20ELEMENTARY

Note: Erroneous disciplinary data for Lorenzo Manor Elementary School.

Reporters at the NBC television station in San Francisco uncovered the erroneous data for Lorenzo Elementary and pressed the state and local administrators for an explanation about how such an error could slip by. The district superintendent said that he didn't have time to review the accuracy of the data. State administrators said they had no independent checks in place and instead relied on the districts to report data accurately. So neither was taking responsibility to ensure accurate data (Susko, Putnam, & Carroll, 2012). Since then, the mistake has been corrected on the Education Department's website.

Journalists at the Reuters news service in New York City discovered big flaws with a national database of hazardous chemical storage that emergency responders use after fires and industrial accidents, such as the April 2013 fertilizer plant explosion in West, Texas. The federal Emergency Planning and Community Right-to-Know Act requires the establishment of state and local networks to plan for emergencies involving hazardous chemicals. In addition, the Act requires facilities to report the presence of hazardous chemicals exceeding certain amounts (Environmental Protection Agency, n.d.a). However, the Reuters news service found that facilities had misreported or failed to report chemicals. Making matters worse, neither federal nor local authorities were checking to make sure the reports were accurate (Pell, McNeill, & Gebrekidan, 2013).

A report ordered by the New York City police commissioner found that the police department's reporting system had poor controls for guarding against intentional manipulation of crime statistics. The report cited several instances of the police downgrading felonies to less serious misdemeanors (Goldstein, 2013).

These might seem like extreme examples, but data flaws are not rare. Government agencies, often compelled by law, collect loads of data. But they don't always set up processes to catch mistakes or run data-integrity checks themselves. That's why we need to be data investigators and look for things like **outliers**, or extreme values that could very well be errors.

ALL DATA ARE DIRTY

One rule to keep in mind is that all data are dirty. But why? How did they get that way?

Dirty data thrive in a number of different environments. As we saw in the examples above, government agencies generated dirty data because of poor or missing controls during the review process. However, if we take a step back we can see that dirty data abound where there are poor controls during the data entry process. It's the old GIGO—garbage in, garbage out—effect.

Think about how data get into a database. As you learned in Chapter 2, in government offices clerical workers often type data from paper forms into a data file. Data-entry clerks usually are low paid and perform this work for hours-long stretches. It's grinding work. Maybe you've entered data as a student worker or for a research project of your own.

It's easy to get distracted and make mistakes. It's also easy, under normal circumstances, to enter data inconsistently. So if a clerk at your city health department is entering data about dog- and other animal-bite complaints, he or she could enter a street as "MacArthur Road", "McArthur Road", "MacArthur Rd.", "McArthur Rd.", "MacArthur Rd", "McArthur Rd" and so on. When you work closely with data, you'll see inconsistencies like these all the time.

Dirty data like these are not just an annoyance—they're also a hindrance. Many computer programs, including spreadsheets, treat each of the six spelling variations above as unique values. So if you want to create a pivot table in your spreadsheet you'll get six rows of data for the same road. Likewise, if you create a chart you'll get six visual elements instead of one.

Applications developers who create Web or computer desktop forms for data entry can build in error-checking tools. Or the forms can limit data input to a set of options. For instance, a form might ask you to pick a city name from a drop-down list. You would have to pick New York instead of typing "NYC", "New York City", "NY", "N.Y." or "N.Y.C." As you can see, constraining choices produces higher-quality data.

Sometimes you'll get data that are dirty or difficult to work with because of how data are stored in columns.

Here's an example: We like to see data about dates like this: month/day/year, so we'd write New Year's Day as 1/1/2015. But the people who create database systems often will store that data as text. So we see 01012015 for New Year's Day. In this case the first 01 stands for the month: January. The second 01 stands for the day of the month. And the last four characters, 2015, are used to record the year.

When someone creates a data file and then chooses to store columns with date data as text, it limits our ability to analyze the file. If the date data are stored as text, we're unable to run date formulas. So we won't be able to do things like calculate the time that has elapsed between dates, or figure out the day of the week based on a date.

Another database design problem that we often grapple with is run-on data. This happens when the person who created the file stuffs more data than we'd like into one column.

Until recently, the Missouri Ethics Commission, the agency that collects and disseminates data about contributions to political campaigns in the state, reported data about contributors in one column. Look at Column G, which is titled ContrInfo, for contributor data.

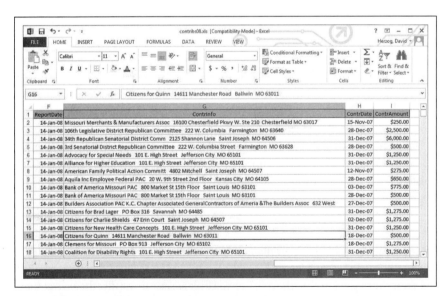

Source: Missouri Ethics Commission, Retrieved from http://www.mec.mo.gov/EthicsWeb/CampaignFinance/CF_ContrCSV.aspx.

Note: Missouri Ethics Commission campaign contribution data. The commission has since improved the structure of the file.

Now this is fine if we'd like to just read it. However, the structure makes it impossible for us to summarize contributions by city, zip code, street address or occupation. Complicating matters more, rows in the column could have data about people, companies or political committees giving money.

As these data stand, we're unable to easily answer questions like, Who is giving the most money? How much money is coming from sources out of state? Are people from particular workplaces making a large number of contributions? From which zip code has the most money come?

You would need to do quite a bit of data scrubbing before you could answer all of those questions definitively. Fortunately, the Missouri Ethics Commission now provides a new version of the data file, one that organizes the individual pieces into columns of their own.

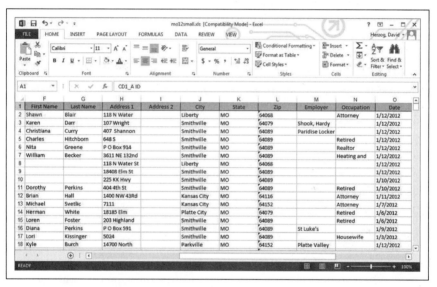

Source: Missouri Ethics Commission. Retrieved from http://www.mec.mo.gov/EthicsWeb/CampaignFinance/CF_ContrCSV.aspx

Note: Improved data from Missouri Ethics Commission.

A huge improvement, right? Committees, companies and individual contributors get their own columns. This would make it easier for us to create sums for each, using pivot tables. In addition, the first and last names get their own columns. Same goes for the street address (two, in fact), city, state and zip code.

Now we could answer the questions that we had posed earlier.

DETECTING DIRT IN AGRICULTURAL DATA

The Food and Agricultural Policy Research Institute at the University of Missouri routinely acquires data from U.S. and foreign government agencies that it uses to make projections about agricultural activity around the world. Established in 1984 with a grant from Congress, FAPRI also uses the data to project the potential impact of agricultural legislation introduced into the U.S. House and Senate.

FAPRI analysts know that the data have flaws and scour them to look for any shortcomings that might have to be corrected or noted, FAPRI director Patrick Westhoff says. (The following discussion is based on Westhoff 2013.) The analysts look over the data in Excel and create charts that help them spot data that are inconsistent or improbable, he says.

Analysts examine supply and use data to see if they are in balance, Westhoff says. That entails making sure the sum of production and imports equals the sum of domestic use, exports and ending stocks. Sometimes FAPRI's agricultural price data are missing information and analysts have to decide whether and how to fill in those missing values, he says.

FAPRI also knows that some data, such as the U.S. Department of Agriculture's estimates of Chinese grain supply and use, can be revised by the provider. Westhoff says that, based on new data, the USDA has several times changed those estimates.

Though FAPRI gets most of its data online, there are times that it manually enters data from published reports or from information obtained on a phone call, something that can lead to human error, Westhoff says.

CHANGED RULES = CHANGED DATA

Changing rules for collecting data can also hurt your data quality, or at least limit your analysis later. Federal government agencies often tweak or even radically change their data collection methods and rules. Following are a few examples from the world of economic data:

Mass layoffs. The Bureau of Labor Statistics began compiling mass layoff statistics starting in 1995. In 2004, it narrowed the scope to cover only private sector, nonfarm workplaces, and no longer counted layoffs in the public and agricultural sectors. So you're unable to accurately compare data from 2004 on with earlier years (Bureau of Labor Statistics, n.d.).

Bankruptcy filings. In 2005 Congress passed and President George W. Bush signed a law that makes it more difficult for some people to file for bankruptcy protection in the federal courts (Public Law 109-8, 2005). As a result, any comparisons of bankruptcy statistics from 2006 on to earlier years would prove inaccurate (United States Courts, n.d.a).

Medical insurance costs. The U.S. Department of Housing and Human Services uses the Medical Expenditure Panel Survey to estimate the cost of single-person and family premiums for employer-based health insurance policies. It's considered the best measure of consumer health-insurance costs. In 2007, however, the survey was put on hold so the DHHS could improve its survey methods. Thus, data for 2007 are missing (Agency for Healthcare Research and Quality, n.d.).

Motor vehicle registrations. The Federal Highway Administration releases data about vehicle registrations by state every year. It collects the data from the state offices that handle the registrations. When the FHWA, which is part of the U.S. Department of Transportation, fails to get numbers from the state authorities, it substitutes numbers from earlier years (Federal Highway Administration, n.d.).

Gross domestic product. The U.S. Bureau of Economic Analysis uses the GDP to measure the size of the U.S. economy, as defined by goods and services. In the summer of 2013 it rewrote "history on a grand scale" by including research and development spending as investments (Coy, 2013). The BEA's move caused the size of the GDP to grow. The BEA recalculated its GDP figures going back to 1929, when the measure was introduced.

As you can see, dirty data are the rule, not the exception. Get used to seeing inconsistencies, typos and misspellings, along with improperly structured data.

Our data are flawed—the question that we need to answer is, How badly are they flawed? In the next chapter, you will learn how you can examine your data so thoroughly that you can make informed and ethical decisions about how to use them. We call this process making data integrity checks.

ON YOUR OWN

Find campaign contribution data for candidates running for state (not U.S.) offices in your state. What problems do you see in your data? Jot down three instances. How do you think these flaws were introduced?

CHAPTER 6 **DATA INTEGRITY CHECKS**

A s we saw in the last chapter, we can expect to find errors in our data. Our next step is to figure out how extensive those errors are.

To do that, we will run **data integrity checks**. Data integrity checks sound pretty daunting, but they really are just a way of systematically examining our data for problems. This chapter will demystify that process and show you how you can use Excel to run the checks.

You're going to learn how to do this using an Excel file that details spending by candidates for the 2012 U.S. Senate race in Texas that was originally downloaded as a comma-separated values (CSV) file from the Federal Election Commission's data portal at http://www.fec.gov/data/CandidateDisbursement.do?format=html&election_yr=2012. You can download this file (TX_all_senate.xls) from the website for this book.

The open seat attracted more than 25 candidates to run in the primary election and was the third-most expensive Congressional race of the 2011–2012 campaign cycle, according to an analysis of FEC data released through April 16, 2013 (OpenSecrets.org, 2014).

When you run data integrity checks you'll need to have your data documentation at your side. Here, it's called the metadata and comes as a webpage at http://www.fec.gov/finance/disclosure/metadata/CandidateDisbursements.shtml. As you learned in Chapter 3, the documentation can go by many other names: record layout, data dictionary, code book and so on.

Practice safe computing by making a copy of the metadata for yourself, so you always have a copy somewhere.

By reading the metadata, we learn that campaigns must report spending when they exceed $200 in payments to a vendor during an election cycle. These data are a good guide for political researchers, campaign operatives and others who want to keep track of candidates' activities. The metadata tell us how frequently candidates file reports and provide guidance about filing amended information for those who submit paper reports, as Senate candidates do.

The FEC also warns us about transactions marked as memo entries, which indicate that the payment was for a credit card bill. The individual payments to vendors using that credit card are listed separately. We want to exclude the memo entries from sums if we analyze the data later so we don't inflate our results.

Pay close attention to the HTML table at the bottom of the page. It contains detailed information about the 26 columns that the FEC provides in the data file.

Information contained in the file

The Candidate disbursement file contains the following information:

Tag	Field Name	Data Type	Description	Range	Explanation
com_id	Committee ID	Character	Character C followed by eight digits	9 characters	Unique nine digit identifier used by the Commission to identify each political committee. In general committee id's begin with the letter C which is followed by eight
com_nam	Committee Name	Character	Name of committee or other entity registered with the FEC	Max 90 characters	This is the name of the committee
can_id	Candidate ID	Character		9 characters	First character indicates office sought - H=House, S=Senate, P=Presidential. Columns 3-4 are the state abbreviation for Congressional candidates
can_nam	Candidate name	Character	Name of the candidate	Max 38 characters	List of all disclosure filings for this committee
ele_yea	Election year	Number		4 characters	General election year of the cycle in which this candidate is running
can_off	Candidate Office	Text	Office abbreviation	1 character	P=President; S=Senate; H=House
can_off_sta	Candidate Office State	Character	Postal abbreviation for State	2 characters	
can_off_dis	Candidate Office District	Number	District number for House candidates	2 characters	
lin_num	Line number from Detailed Summary Page of FEC Form 3	Character	category of disbursement based on detailed summary page of FEC Form 3	max 12 characters	Description of Form 3 (See page 6 of these instructions)
lin_ima	Link to image presentation	URI	Page where transaction may be viewed as image	11 characters	
rec_com_id	Recipient Committee ID	Character	Character C followed by eight digits	9 characters	If the disbursement goes to another committee registered with the FEC, this would be the ID number of the committee receiving the payment

Source: Federal Election Commission, Retrieved from http://www.fec.gov/finance/disclosure/metadata/CandidateDisbursements .shtml.

Note: Documentation for Federal Election Commission expenditure data.

Tag tells us what the column is named in the data file.

Field Name is a longer, more-descriptive name for the column.

Data Type shows the data format. You'll see that ele_yea, the election year, is stored as a number.

Description provides details about the contents of the column.

Range tells the number of spaces for the data in each column.

Explanation has even more details about the contents of the column.

TX_all_senate

Source: Microsoft Excel for Windows 2013.

Note: Icon for Excel file with federal campaign spending data.

BIG-PICTURE CHECKS

Immediately after we get a file, we want to answer a few big-picture questions before moving on to running the more-detailed data-integrity checks. We need to ask,

What is the file format?

How many rows do we have?

Are all of the columns present with proper headers?

So go ahead and find the file on your computer. Look at the icon for it and make sure it's a Microsoft Excel spreadsheet file. On a Windows computer, you can also look for the file extension. The extension .xls means it's an Excel 1997–2003 workbook.

Open the file TX_all_senate.xls with Excel and you'll see this:

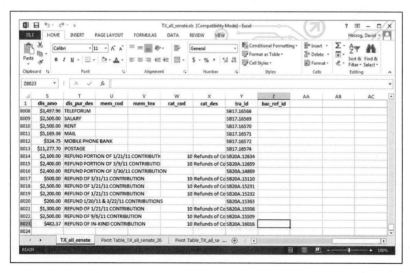

Source: Federal Election Commission.

Note: Federal campaign spending data for Texas open in Excel.

Let's answer our second question: How many rows does the file have? We answer that by telling Excel to go to the end of the sheet by clicking Ctrl-End on our keyboard (Command-End if you are using a Mac). Now we're at cell Z8023, or the very far right end of the sheet. So you have 8,023 rows, or 8,022 rows with data plus one header.

Source: Federal Election Commission.

Note: End of data in federal campaign spending Excel file.

Scroll left to get to the A column. Now hit Ctrl-Home (or Command-Home) and you've returned to the top of your spreadsheet.

Now for the third check: Look at the column headers in Row 1 and make sure they are the same as in the metadata. It's tempting to change the headers to something that's more meaningful to us. However, it's best to practice safe computing by keeping the original names. That way, anyone who works with the data can easily refer to the metadata.

They do match and we're ready to move on to the next step: Data integrity checks for each column.

DETAILED CHECKS

For these checks we will generate **pivot tables** that list each data value and the number of times that value appears. You'll see quickly that these checks let us take a good look at what we have to work with.

Let's start with the com_id column, which has nine characters and is used by the FEC to uniquely identify candidates. Each should start with one character, followed by eight digits.

Here's how to start the pivot table:

1. Make sure your cursor is clicked inside one of the cells with data.
2. Select the Insert tab and then the Pivot Table button.
3. Excel asks you to Choose the data you would like to analyze. Excel should automatically pick Select a table or range and highlight the data. Put the results into a new worksheet.
4. Click OK

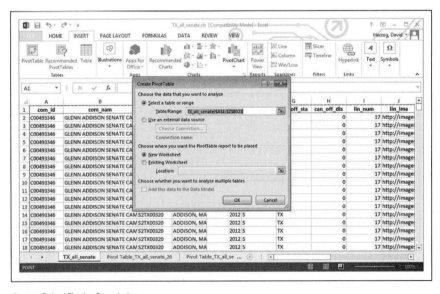

Source: Federal Election Commission.

Note: Create pivot table dialog box in Excel.

Now Excel opens the pivot table designer.

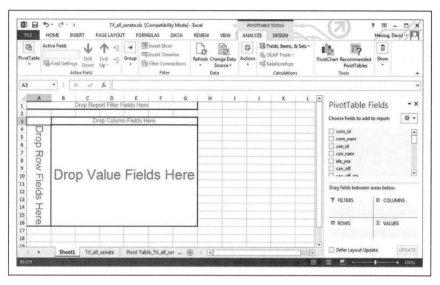

Source: Microsoft Excel for Windows 2013.

Note: Excel pivot table designer. Use this blank form to create a pivot table.

The PivotTable Fields selector on the right lists the headers for all of the columns in our data. So you can see there an entry for com_id, the committee ID. The layout area on the left gives us boxes for creating our pivot tables.

Getting started is as simple as dragging a field name and dropping it on the layout. We want to make a pivot table for the com_id, so drag that field over to the ROWS box. We want to see the IDs listed in our column to the left.

Next, we want to create a column to the right that shows how many times each com_id appears in the data. So let's drag the com_id from the list into the VALUES box. Excel, by default, says that it wants to count what we put in VALUES box. It's smart enough to know that we can't sum or average the com_id because the contents of the field are text, not numbers. Excel then generates this pivot table report:

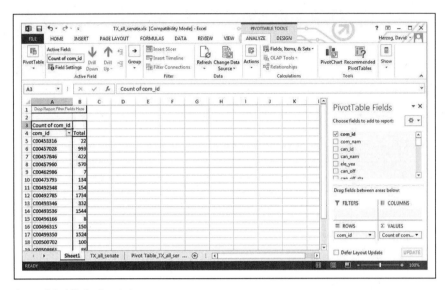

Source: Federal Election Commission.

Note: Pivot table counting com_id entries. Each com_id entry is listed, along with the number of times it appears in the file.

We see 17 unique committee IDs, along with the number of items associated with each committee in the data file. They are listed in ascending order. We also see a total of 8,022, which we recall is the total number of lines of data that we have. Finally, we see that all of the com_id numbers start with one character and end with eight digits, just as the metadata said.

So this column checks out fine.

Make a note in your data notebook that 25 candidates ran for the Senate seat, so we are eight committees short. We could speculate that the other eight failed to spend enough money to meet the reporting threshold, but we would need to verify that.

Change the name of the Excel worksheet tab from "Sheet" to "com_id IC", for com_id integrity check. That way you'll know what's on this tab. (Do this for all of your pivot table sheets.)

Practice safe computing: We've made changes to our sheet, so let's preserve the original and create a new, working version. Save a working version of the file by picking File | Save As . . . Excel should remember that the file type is Excel 1997–2003 and the original file name. You can add the number "1" to the file name, making this version TX_all_senate1. After working with data for a while you will no doubt adopt a file-naming convention that fits your workflow.

Now, let's run a data integrity check on the com_nam. We had 17 entries in the com_id field, so we would expect to see the same number when we count the names.

Run a pivot table to check for sure. (You'll need to return to the main sheet holding the data to do this.)

	A	B
2		
3	Count of com_nam	
4	com_nam	Total
5	CAS FOR SENATE	7
6	COMMITTEE TO ELECT LELA PITTENGER FOR UNITED STATES SENATE	134
7	CRAIG JAMES FOR UNITED STATES SENATE	233
8	DEWHURST FOR TEXAS	1524
9	ELIZABETH AMES JONES FOR TEXAS INC	993
10	FLORENCE SHAPIRO FOR TEXAS INC	22
11	GARZA FOR TEXAS EXPLORATORY COMMITTEE	8
12	GLENN ADDISON SENATE CAMPAIGN	332
13	HUBBARD FOR SENATE CAMPAIGN	154
14	JASON GIBSON FOR US SENATE	9
15	MICHAEL WILLIAMS FOR CONGRESS	570
16	PAUL SADLER FOR SENATE	86
17	PEOPLE FOR CURT CLEAVER; THE	100
18	ROGER WILLIAMS FOR US SENATE COMMITTEE	422
19	SANCHEZ FOR SENATE	150
20	TED CRUZ FOR SENATE	1734
21	TEXANS FOR TOM LEPPERT	1544
22	Grand Total	8022

Source: Federal Election Commission.

Note: Pivot table showing com_nam and how many times each appears.

All is well because we have 17 unique committee names and the grand total adds up to 8,022 at the bottom.

Our next integrity check will be on can_id, which the metadata says should be nine characters. The first character indicates the race, and the third and fourth indicate the state. So we will expect to see "S" then "TX".

	A	B
2		
3	Count of can_id	
4	can_id	Total
5	S0TX00134	22
6	S0TX00142	570
7	S0TX00175	7
8	S0TX00217	134
9	S2TX00262	993
10	S2TX00270	422
11	S2TX00304	154
12	S2TX00312	1734
13	S2TX00320	332
14	S2TX00338	1544
15	S2TX00346	8
16	S2TX00353	150
17	S2TX00361	1524
18	S2TX00387	100
19	S2TX00411	233
20	S2TX00429	86
21	S2TX00437	9
22	Grand Total	8022

Source: Federal Election Commission.

Note: Pivot table showing can_ids and how many times each appears.

That check confirms our thinking. Again, we have 17 candidates listed (one tied to each committee) and 8,022 total count.

Along the same lines, we want to check the cand_name, which lists the names of the candidates. We should see 17, with a total count of 8,022.

	A	B
2		
3	Count of can_nam	
4	can_nam ▼	Total
5	ADDISON, MARSHALL GLENN	332
6	CASTANUELA, ANDREW PAREDES	7
7	CLEAVER, CURTIS C	100
8	CRUZ, RAFAEL EDWARD TED	1734
9	DEWHURST, DAVID H	1524
10	GARZA, STANLEY	8
11	GIBSON, JASON AARON	9
12	HUBBARD, SEAN PETER	154
13	JAMES, CRAIG	233
14	JONES, ELIZABETH AMES	993
15	LEPPERT, THOMAS C	1544
16	PITTENGER, LELA MAE	134
17	SADLER, PAUL LINDSEY	86
18	SANCHEZ, RICARDO SAUCEDA	150
19	SHAPIRO, FLORENCE	22
20	WILLIAMS, MICHAEL L	570
21	WILLIAMS, ROGER	422
22	Grand Total	8022

Source: Federal Election Commission.

Note: Pivot table of can_nam, showing the candidate names and how many times each appears.

That's exactly what we have above.

Next is ele_yea, or the election year. Since all of these candidates were running in the 2012 election, we should see only that date after our integrity check. Excel sums the years, because they are stored as numbers, so we need to go into the pivot table settings and tell Excel to count instead.

3	Sum of ele_yea		
4	ele_yea	▾	Total
5		2012	16140264
6	Grand Total		16140264

Source: Federal Election Commission.

Note: Pivot table showing ele_yea or year of the election. Excel sums the year values, which gives inaccurate results.

We can change that by selecting the drop-down arrow on the Values box at the lower right, then picking value field settings. Using the box that appears, we can now select Count.

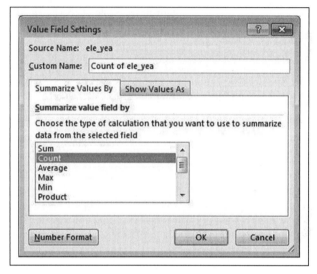

Source: Microsoft Excel for Windows 2013.

Note: Change to count in value field settings.

It worked! We now see that 2012 appears 8,022 times.

3	Count of ele_yea		
4	ele_yea	▾	Total
5		2012	8022
6	Grand Total		8022

Source: Federal Election Commission.

Note: Count of ele_year. Now Excel reports accurate number. All of the entries are 2012, as expected.

The data integrity check for can_off, the office sought by the candidate, is next. We have data about U.S. Senate candidates only, so we shouldn't see "H" for U.S. House or "P" for president at all.

3	Count of can_off		
4	can_off	▼	Total
5	S		8022
6	Grand Total		8022

Source: Federal Election Commission.

Note: Pivot table for can_off column.

3	Count of can_off_sta		
4	can_off_sta	▼	Total
5	TX		8022
6	Grand Total		8022

Source: Federal Election Commission.

Note: Pivot table with results for can_off_sta results.

Our next couple of checks, for the state of the race (can_off_sta) and the district (can_off_dis), likewise should generate no surprises. We should see "TX" for the state and 0 for the district (because there are no districts for U.S. Senate races: they're statewide contests).

3	Sum of can_off_dis		
4	can_off_dis	▼	Total
5		0	0
6	Grand Total		0

Source: Federal Election Commission.

Note: Pivot table with results for can_off_dis column. All the entries are "0" because the data are for the Senate contests, not House races.

Lin_num refers to the line number for the detailed summary page for FEC Form 3, which is used to gather these data from the campaign committees. The line on the form contains summary information, so any item listed as a row in the spreadsheet is a component of that.

Count of lin_num		
lin_num	▼	Total
	17	7568
	18	3
	21	7
19A		32
19B		8
20A		399
20C		5
Grand Total		8022

Source: Federal Election Commission.

Note: Pivot table with lin_num results.

Excel lists seven different values, with 17 having the greatest number. Note that Excel justifies data values stored as numbers to the right and those stored as text to the left. (If we wanted, we could have formatted the entire column as text to avoid this annoying feature.)

We need more help in decoding what this all means, so we follow the Description of Form 3 link in the metadata and find a PDF document that explains what summary data go on each line. Committees use instructions located at http://www.fec.gov/pdf/forms/fecfrm3i.pdf when filing their reports.

On page 7 of the documentation, the FEC tells us that Line 17 is supposed to summarize all operating expenses of committees and to provide details on what that covers. The FEC has instructions for the other lines here, too.

The next column, lin_ima, contains a URL that links to an image showing the spending item from the original report filed by the committees. We don't need to perform any checks because we wouldn't perform any analysis on this column, but would just use the links later for looking up details.

The next column, rec_com_id, is used to identify other committees that might receive money from our candidate committees for U.S. Senate in Texas. The committee IDs are nine characters, starting with one letter.

3	Count of rec_com_id	
4	rec_com_id	Total
5	C00143743	1
6	C00310532	1
7	C00326835	1
8	C00355461	1
9	C00457960	167
10	C00498121	3
11	S0TX00217	24
12	S2TX00270	3
13	S2TX00312	1
14	S2TX00338	2
15	S2TX00361	1
16	S2TX00411	1
17	(blank)	
18	Grand Total	206

Source: Federal Election Commission.

Note: Results for rec_com_id column.

Interesting: out of our 8,022 total records, only a fraction (206) are for committee disbursements to other committees. A dozen other committee ID numbers turn up in our check. You could punch these into the FEC's committee advanced search at http://www.fec.gov/finance/disclosure/advcomsea.shtml. That tells us the first listed (C00143743) is for the Republican Party of Texas.

So far, our integrity checks have generated pretty compact pivot tables because the columns that we've looked at had little variation in terms of data values. That's about to change with the next column, for the name of the recipient (rec_nam).

Now, if we scroll to the bottom of our pivot table, we see we have around 1,780 entries, with all 8,022 records accounted for.

	A	B
1771	WOODALL, CYNTHIA	1
1772	WOODFOREST NAT'L BANK	1
1773	WOODS, TOM	7
1774	WOOT.COM INC	1
1775	WORLD MAGAZINE	1
1776	WORLEY PRINTING CO, INC.	2
1777	WORTHINGTON, CHRIS	1
1778	WRIGHT, ROBERT J MR	1
1779	WXXV	1
1780	WYATT, JEANIE	1
1781	WYNN LAS VEGAS	3
1782	YELLOW CAB	10
1783	YORK, PAUL W	1
1784	ZEIDMAN, FRED S	1
1785	7/11/2012	2
1786	Grand Total	8022

Source: Federal Election Commission.

Note: Dirty data in the rec_nam column. Note the date at the bottom.

Now zip back to the top of the pivot table. We notice, for the first time, that we have a *lot* of dirty data.

Here are some examples:

"ADOBE SYSTEMS" and "ADOBE SYSTEM, INC."

"ADVANTAGE RENT A CAR" and "ADVANTAGE RENT-A-CAR"

Scroll down to find "AIRTRAN" and "AIRTRAN AIRWAYS"

At this point, it's easy to see how cleaning data can be a big job. A lot of people ask, Do I really need to clean everything up? Here, the answer is yes, if you wanted to definitively be able to tell which vendor received the greatest number of payments or the most money.

As with the vendor names, we can expect a lot of variation and dirt to appear in our integrity checks of the recipient street address columns (rec_str1 and rec_str2).

And so there is. Our check of rec_str_1 turns up some of these errors or inconsistencies:

We have a number of blanks: 7,846 rows in this column have addresses.

We have a number of PO boxes, which are not physical addresses.

Street directional prefixes sometimes are spelled out, and sometimes are abbreviated ("STREET" vs. "ST").

We get many fewer rows in our check of rec_str_2. For one thing, committees do not fill it out as often as rect_str_1. Here is what we find in terms of dirty data:

PO boxes are listed in this column, too.

"Suite" is spelled out sometimes, abbreviated others.

"Floor" is spelled out sometimes, abbreviated others.

Now we do checks for rec_cit and rec_state, so we can see the location of the person, company or committee that got the payment.

Our check of rec_cit tells us:

We have 289 distinct values listed;

The vast majority of records have city data: 7,887 in all;

The city names are pretty consistent; and that

We do have some errors: "FORT WORTHZ" and "FT WORTHS" for Fort Worth.

Our check of rec_sta reveals payments went to 39 states; and all the states are listed properly.

This might not be the best way to test the integrity of our locations, though. Cities don't stand alone—they're part of states, right? We can use pivot tables to combine cities and states in our results. It's a little more complicated than the pivot tables we've been building so far. Let's walk through the steps.

Start the pivot table and add rec_cit to your rows. Then add rec_sta to your rows and make sure it's under rec_cit. Put rec_cit into the Data Fields area and make sure it's set to Count. Your pivot table builder should look like this:

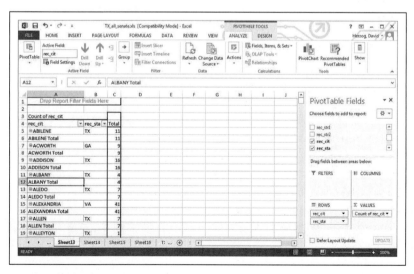

Source: Federal Election Commission.

Note: Pivot table with more than two rows for categories.

731	⊟WASHINGTON	DC	135
732		TX	1
733	WASHINGTON Total		136

Source: Federal Election Commission.

Note: Detail of city and state pivot table.

It's a little confusing, because Excel also tells us, under each city, how many times each city appears. We can see this better by scrolling down to Washington.

Much better, isn't it? We can see that we have an Amarillo in Tennessee, which could very well be a typo. Farther down the list, we see "Pittsburg" (missing an h) in Pennsylvania, an obvious misspelling that we'd want to clean up before we used the city column for analysis.

Our last address column check is rec_zip for the zip code of the recipient.

3	Count of rec_zip	
4	rec_zip ▼	Total
5	1702	8
6	2118	3
7	2241	2
8	2451	3
9	3302	17
10	3449	4
11	4101	4
12	6103	3
13	6115	3
14	6461	1
15	6824	5
16	6854	5
17	6878	1
18	6902	1

Source: Federal Election Commission.

Note: Pivot table for rec_zip.

Straightaway we spot some problems—namely zip codes with only four characters. That's in conflict with our metadata, which says a zip may have five or nine characters.

Let's go back to our original sheet with the data and sort it by rec_zip, so we can get a better picture of what the problem is. Practice safe computing: Select the entire sheet by clicking on the button between A and 1. This highlights everything and tells Excel that you want to keep your rows together while sorting.

Pick the Data tab and then the big Sort button. You get this dialog box, which allows you to control how Excel sorts the sheet.

Make sure the My data has headers box is checked because this tells Excel to use the header names in the Sort by drop-down list. Pick rec_zip and Smallest to Largest in the Order drop-down list. Excel should look like this on your screen:

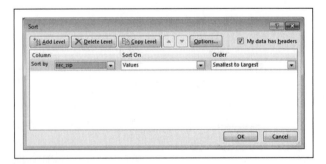

Source: Federal Election Commission.

Note: Excel sort dialog box.

All the zip codes with four characters are from New England or New Jersey. Those zip codes in real life all have leading zeroes, which somehow got stripped out of our data. We would need to add those if we wanted to use the zip column for any analysis. We might also want to extract five-character zip codes from the ones with nine characters, to keep our data consistent.

Our next couple of checks will be handy in looking for suspect values. These are outliers, or numbers that are so extreme that they might be incorrect. Suspect values often pop up in columns that contain dates or numbers.

The dis_dat column tells us the date that the disbursement was made. Because this comes from the 2012 federal election cycle, we expect all will be from the start of 2011 through the end of 2012.

Our check reveals some flawed data that we see right at the top of our list. Namely, one instance of 1/1/1916—a date in the far past! Next, the dates start with January 1, 2011, just as we expected. A check of the bottom of the pivot table shows all of the entries end within our expected time frame.

Now for the amount of disbursement in the dis_amo column.

3	Count of dis_dat	
4	dis_dat ▼	Total
5	1/1/1916	1
6	1/1/2011	3
7	1/2/2011	1
8	1/4/2011	4
9	1/5/2011	1

Source: Federal Election Commission.

Note: Integrity check for dis_dat column. This shows we have an outlier, a date that's so far in the past that it's no doubt an error.

3	Count of dis_amo	
4	dis_amo ▼	Total
5	-2400	1
6	-1503	1
7	-500	2
8	-200	2
9	-169	1
10	-150	1
11	-149.17	1
12	-100	1
13	-79	1
14	-50	1
15	-35	1
16	-10	1
17	-1.13	1
18	-1	1
19	0.01	2

Source: Federal Election Commission.

Note: Dis_amo integrity check. Negative numbers are often used by the Federal Election Commission to indicate refunds.

At first, you might think these results are odd—how can committees have negative spending amounts? But if you are familiar with the FEC's data, you know that negative amounts are often used to denote refunds. They could be money that vendors returned to campaigns, or they could be typos.

At the other end of our amount, we see two payments exceeding $1 million. That's a lot compared to most of the other amounts, so we would want to look more closely at those.

Our next column (dis_pur_des) sets aside 100 characters for the campaigns to add free-form descriptions of the reason for the spending. So we expect that we'll get a lot of variation and overlap.

77	BALLOT ACCESS FEE	1
78	BANK CHARGE	3
79	BANK CHARGES	9
80	BANK FEE	144
81	BANK FEES	3
82	BANK SEE CHARGE	1
83	BANK SERVICE CHARGE	1
84	BANK SERVICE CHARGES	2
85	BANK SERVICE CHARGES, MEALS (SEE BELOW I	1
86	BANK SERVICE FEE	14
87	BANKING FEE	2
88	BANNER	1
89	BANNERS	2
90	BATCHING/CAGING	1
91	BEVERAGE - FUNDRAISER	1
92	BEVERAGE & WAIT PERSONS FOR FUNDRAISER	1

Source: Federal Election Commission.

Note: Integrity check for dis_pur_des column. These results show a lack of standardization in how this column is filled out.

Indeed, there are many ways that campaigns have entered bank fee disbursements, for example. We'd need to scrub this column a lot in order to use it.

3	Count of mem_cod	
4	mem_cod ▾	Total
5	X	718
6	(blank)	
7	Grand Total	718

Source: Federal Election Commission.

Note: Mem_cod integrity check.

Mem_cod, the next column, is important because it tells us whether the data stored in a row hold details from a credit card payment. An "x" indicates an itemized payment that's also accounted for in a credit card payment. If we analyze the data, we'd want to make sure that we're not double-summing or double-counting these items.

The pivot table tells us that we have 718 memo entries whose dollar amounts are also included in the credit card payment. An integrity check of the mem_tex column, used to store more-detailed data about the memo, shows us this:

3	Count of mem_tex	
4	mem_tex	Total
5	* IN-KIND RECEIVED	16
6	[MEMO ITEM]	582
7	[MEMO ITEM] SUBITEMIZATION OF AMERICAN EXPRESS(02/16/11)	4
8	[MEMO ITEM] SUBITEMIZATION OF CARD SERVICE CENTER(02/20/12)	5
9	[MEMO ITEM] SUBITEMIZATION OF CARD SERVICE CENTER(03/22/12)	8
10	[MEMO ITEM] SUBITEMIZATION OF CARD SERVICE CENTER(04/18/12)	7
11	[MEMO ITEM] SUBITEMIZATION OF CARD SERVICE CENTER(05/18/12)	6
12	[MEMO ITEM] SUBITEMIZATION OF FASKEN MANAGEMENT LLC(12/29/1	1
13	[MEMO ITEM] SUBITEMIZATION OF VIRGINIA BELL(01/29/11)	3
14	ACCOUNTING SERVICES	5
15	BANK CHARGES	1
16	CONTRIBUTION	1
17	FOOD/BEVERAGE	1

Source: Federal Election Commission.

Note: Mem_tex integrity check.

Most of the entries are "[MEMO ITEM]", with 582. We'd have to explore individual records more to make sense of this.

The cat_cod column is supposed to hold a code with a value from 001 to 012 that categorizes the reason for the disbursement. As it did with zip codes, Excel stripped the leading zeroes. That's not a big problem here. But we see 12 entries for 0 and eight entries for 17, which are outside our range of values, and some for "ENT" and "IND", which are not listed in the metadata. We also see that 005 and 008 do not appear in our data, leaving us with 10 valid codes in all.

3	Count of cat_cod	
4	cat_cod	Total
5	0	12
6	1	975
7	2	293
8	3	59
9	4	209
10	6	46
11	7	103
12	9	27
13	10	208
14	11	8
15	12	2
16	17	8
17	ENT	59
18	IND	60
19	(blank)	
20	Grand Total	2069

Source: Federal Election Commission.

Note: Integrity check for cat_cod column.

A check of cat_des provides a list of the descriptions behind the codes.

3	Count of cat_des	
4	cat_des	Total
5	Administrative/Salary/Overhead Expenses	975
6	Advertising Expenses	209
7	Campaign Event Expenses	103
8	Campaign Materials	46
9	Donations	2
10	Loan Repayments	27
11	Political Contributions	8
12	Refunds of Contributions	208
13	Solicitation and Fundraising Expenses	59
14	Travel Expenses	293
15	(blank)	
16	Grand Total	1930

Source: Federal Election Commission.

Note: Cat_des integrity check

We get 10 descriptions, which match the 10 valid codes on our earlier check.
We could have included the cat_code and cat_des together to get an even better look.

3	Count of cat_cod			
4	cat_cod		cat_des	Total
5		⊟0	(blank)	12
6	0 Total			12
7		⊟1	Administrative/Salary/Overhead Expenses	975
8	1 Total			975
9		⊟2	Travel Expenses	293
10	2 Total			293
11		⊟3	Solicitation and Fundraising Expenses	59
12	3 Total			59
13		⊟4	Advertising Expenses	209
14	4 Total			209
15		⊟6	Campaign Materials	46
16	6 Total			46
17		⊟7	Campaign Event Expenses	103
18	7 Total			103
19		⊟9	Loan Repayments	27
20	9 Total			27
21		⊟10	Refunds of Contributions	208

Source: Federal Election Commission.

Note: Cat_cod and cat_des integrity check. Adding the columns together provides a more comprehensive look.

Coming around to our last checks, we expect to see unique values in the tra_id column, which is the transaction identification number. We can find the multiples by creating the pivot table normally, then sorting the Count column descending, to put the biggest counts at the top. Do that by right-clicking on any number in the Count column, then picking Sort | Sort Largest to Smallest.

Our check shows several dozen IDs that have duplicates. We'd want to question the FEC about that.

3	Count of tra_id	
4	tra_id	Total
5	SB0427100212703	2
6	SB05101005126	2
7	SB0427100212711	2
8	SB0427100212673	2
9	SB0427100212699	2
10	SB0427100212674	2
11	SB0427100212707	2
12	SB0427100212675	2
13	SB051010051212	2
14	SB0427100212676	2
15	SB0427100212697	2
16	SB0427100212677	2
17	SB0427100212701	2

Source: Federal Election Commission.

Note: Tra_id integrity check.

The bac_ref_id, our last check, is used to identify whether a transaction is part of a larger credit card transaction. This shows we have 95 records that are part of larger transactions.

3	Count of bac_ref_id	
4	bac_ref_id	Total
5	SB17.12598	18
6	SB17.14042	8
7	SB17.14076	2
8	SB17.14114	8
9	SB17.14717	1
10	SB17.14735	1
11	SB17.14741	45
12	SB17.15201	5
13	SB17.15235	1
14	SB17.15241	5
15	SB17.15496	1
16	(blank)	
17	Grand Total	95

Source: Federal Election Commission.

Note: Bac_ref_id integrity check.

Running data integrity checks can be an exhaustive (and exhausting) process. But by doing these checks, we get to know our data inside and out. To recap, our data integrity checks here unmasked inconsistencies in the names and addresses of recipients. We also discovered some negative numbers, which are probably refunds.

As students or professionals who use data to create information and knowledge, it's important for us to know these data's strengths and shortcomings.

In the next chapter we will learn how to clean our data so we can analyze and visualize them later with confidence.

ON YOUR OWN

Download a copy of the 2014 disbursements files for the U.S. Senate candidates in your state from the FEC data portal at http://www.fec.gov/data/CandidateDisbursement.do and run integrity checks. Keep notes in your data notebook. What problems do you see? How would these problems impair your analysis?

CHAPTER 7 GETTING YOUR DATA IN SHAPE

I n the previous chapter, we learned how to use integrity checks to uncover flaws in our data. In this chapter we will learn some tricks that we can use to scrub some of the most common data dirt. We will also learn some techniques for transforming our data, so they are better prepared for analysis and visualization.

We will use Excel to perform most of our data cleaning and transforming tasks, but we will also use OpenRefine and a PDF conversion service.

Excel and other spreadsheet programs have built-in features and functions that can help whip data into shape. For example, we can use Excel's Text to Columns tool to **parse**—or split—data that are stored in one column into multiple columns. This is useful when we have a column for full names that are stored like, "Doe, Jane". Using **Text to Columns**, we could carve this into one column for the last name, and another column for the first name. Excel also has a Remove Duplicates tool that allows us to remove rows that hold data that are repeated. In addition, we can write formulas in our Excel spreadsheets to carve out data and then assemble them. This is handy when we have dates stored as text, such as "20150101" for January 1, 2015.

OpenRefine (which runs on Windows, Mac and Linux computers) is an open-source program from Google that lets users quickly run data integrity checks, then clean flawed data. Its creators call it a power tool for working with messy data (http://openrefine.org).

Cometdocs and Zamzar are two online converters that allow us to extract Excel files from PDF tables.

Then there are even more-powerful and more-complex tools for data cleaning that are outside the scope of this book. More-advanced data users will use database managers, such as Microsoft Access or MySQL, to clean data using string functions. String functions are code that can be inserted into the **Structured Query Language** (SQL) that these database managers execute. For instance, someone who's adept with SQL can write queries to rearrange dates into a proper format and put them into a new column. Data users who are even more advanced write scripts using programming languages like **Python**, **Ruby**, PHP or **Perl** to clean and transform data sets. These programming languages allow users to process huge amounts of data more quickly than they could using traditional programs like database managers and spreadsheets. In addition, a number of companies offer data cleaning services and software.

For a deeper look at data cleaning, check out the *Bad Data Handbook* (McCallum, 2012) or *Best Practices in Data Cleaning* (Osborne, 2013), which is geared to working with primary data collected for the purposes of research.

There's plenty that we can do, though, with Excel, PDF converters and OpenRefine, so we'll start to tackle some of the most common challenges now.

COLUMN CARVING

Government agencies often stuff too much data into one column, which makes it difficult for us to work with them. In Chapter 5, we took a look at political campaign contribution data from the Missouri Ethics Commission that stores all the identifying data about contributors into one column. This is an extreme example of dirty data. Someone with advanced data-cleaning skills might be able to parse these data elements into separate fields, but that would take a lot of work. As shown in that chapter, the commission now provides these data with the data broken down into multiple columns that users can work with better.

Most column parsing challenges are far simpler, such as the one in our spreadsheet of dangerous dogs that have been reported to animal control authorities in the city of Austin, Texas. The city's Animal Services Office allows people to fill out forms asserting that a dog is dangerous or has bitten another animal (AustinTexas.gov, n.d.). The original file has been modified for this exercise. The file is called Austin_Declared_Dangerous_Dogs.xlsx and has 40 rows, including one for the column headers. (You should have your data notebook open so you can record any activities.)

We see four columns, one each for the street address, zip code, description of the dog and the dog's location, which includes latitude and longitude points that someone

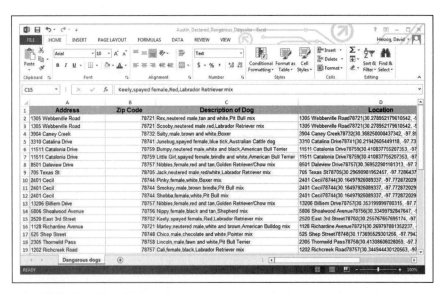

Source: Retrieved from Data.austintexas.gov.

Note: Austin declared dangerous dog data. Note the Description of Dog column has four pieces of data, separated by a comma.

could use to create a webmap. The Description of Dog column has a lot of different bits of data mashed together: the dog's name, sex, color and breed. Each piece of data is separated by a comma, a pattern that is important to note before using the Text to Columns tool.

Let's get ready by saving a copy of the spreadsheet with a name other than the original, so we preserve the original copy. We will work with the new file.

If we use Text to Columns, it will overwrite our original data in Column C. We want to preserve that for reference, so insert four columns to the right of Column C. We'll need four columns because we're going to parse out four data items. Right-click on Column D and pick Insert from the popup menu four times. You should have blank columns from D through G.

Practice safe computing by copying the contents of Column C into Column D: Right-click on C and pick Copy from the popup menu, then right-click on D and pick Paste. Your spreadsheet should look like this with Column D highlighted:

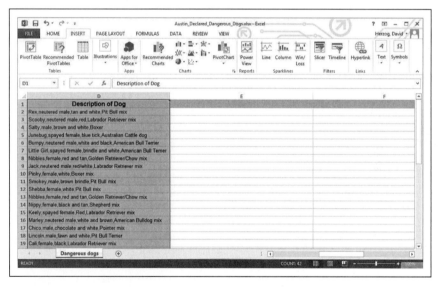

Source: Retrieved from Data.austintexas.gov.

Note: Description of Dog column, ready for parsing.

Now we're ready to tell Excel to perform its magic. Click on the Data tab and then the Text to Columns button. Excel launches a Wizard that walks us through carving up the data in three steps. In the first step, tell Excel the correct data type, which is delimited.

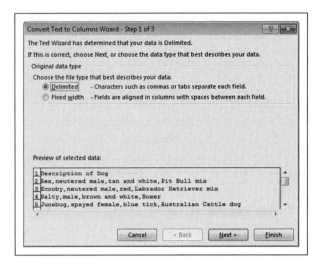

Source: Microsoft Excel for Windows 2013.

Note: Step 1 of the Text to Columns Wizard for delimited data.

Click Next and it's time to set more options. We need to tell Excel that the delimiter is a comma, so make sure only that box is checked in the Delimiters section. We have no text qualifiers (single or double quotation marks to denote text), so change that to None. In the preview area, Excel draws lines where the column breaks will go, based on the position of the comma delimiters.

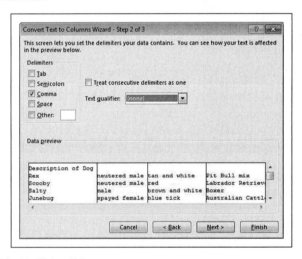

Source: Microsoft Excel for Windows 2013.

Note: Step 2 of the Text to Columns Wizard for delimited data.

Click Next and we're in the last step of our wizard, where we set the data types for the four columns that we are creating. Change all of these from General to Text. Do that by selecting all of the headers, which say General, and changing the Column data format to Text. Click Finish and Excel carves up the data into four columns. If you get a warning about overwriting existing data, click OK. That's just Excel's way of telling you that the data in Column D will be modified. (This is why we saved the original in Column C.)

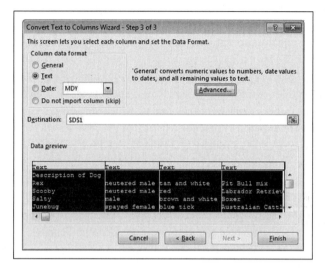

Note: Step 3 of the Text to Columns wizard for delimited data.

Note: Parsed Description of Dog column. Note that each of the four pieces of data is stored in its own column.

So Column D holds the name of the dog, Column E the sex and whether it's been neutered or spayed, F the color and G the breed. Now that we've placed the breed of the dog in its own column, we could create an Excel pivot table that tells us which breed is the most common on the dangerous dogs list. Let's practice safe computing by adding some labels that make sense: Change the contents of cell D1 to "name", E1 to "sex", F1 to "color" and G1 to "breed". Now save the file and close it because we are done with it for now.

Carving up data using Text to Columns usually is more complicated than this because of the way government agencies store data. Get the Excel file fuel_economy2013.xlsx from the book website and open it. Make a working copy using File I Save As. This file from the U.S Department of Energy and the Environmental Protection Agency lists fuel economy data for vehicles that are sold in the United States. The data are in 1,166 rows, including one for the headers. Let's scroll over to column AC, which provides descriptive data about each vehicle's drive system. The first line tells us that the drive system for one particular variant of the Aston Martin V8 Vantage is "2-Wheel Drive, Rear". That's actually two pieces of data: the drive system is two-wheel and those two wheels are the rear ones. We could use the comma and space that follows it to carve this into two distinct columns.

Using Insert, create two new columns, one for the number of wheels and the other to designate which wheels propel the vehicle. Copy the contents of AC and paste them into AD. Make sure AD is highlighted and start the Text to Columns Function.

Choose delimited in the first screen of the wizard and pick Next.

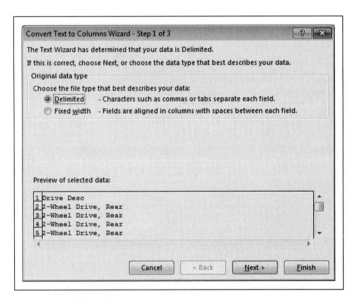

Source: Microsoft Excel for Windows 2013.

Note: Step 1 in the Text to Columns wizard for delimited data.

Set the delimiter to Comma only and make sure text qualifier is None. Excel gives a preview of how it's going to parse the data. Look closely and you will see that Excel is including the spaces on either side of the comma as text. That's OK for now. We'll fix that later.

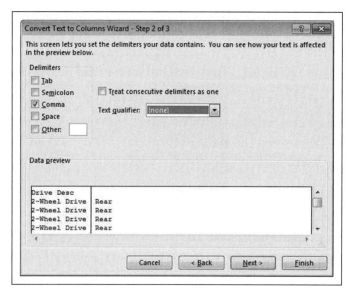

Note: Step 2 in the Text to Columns wizard for delimited data.

Click Next to move on to the third and final step. Change both of these columns to Text and then Finish.

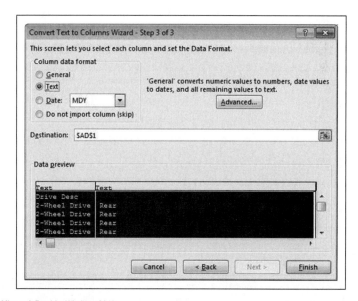

Note: Step 3 in the Text to Columns wizard for delimited data.

This is great—Excel has carved the data up in Columns AD and AE. Label AD "NumWheels" (for number of wheels) and AE "DriveWheels".

AC	AD	AE
Drive Desc	Drive Desc	
2-Wheel Drive, Rear	2-Wheel Drive	Rear
2-Wheel Drive, Rear	2-Wheel Drive	Rear
2-Wheel Drive, Rear	2-Wheel Drive	Rear
2-Wheel Drive, Rear	2-Wheel Drive	Rear
All Wheel Drive	All Wheel Drive	
2-Wheel Drive, Rear	2-Wheel Drive	Rear
2-Wheel Drive, Rear	2-Wheel Drive	Rear
2-Wheel Drive, Rear	2-Wheel Drive	Rear
2-Wheel Drive, Rear	2-Wheel Drive	Rear
2-Wheel Drive, Rear	2-Wheel Drive	Rear
All Wheel Drive	All Wheel Drive	

Source: Department of Energy.

Note: Data parsed, but with extraneous spaces.

Our next step is to remove those extraneous spaces using Excel. We want to remove these because the spaces technically are data (one of the basic ASCII characters) and could throw off any analysis. Column AE has leading spaces in the cells. We have "Rear" or "Front" for the values, when we really want no leading spaces in them. Excel's TRIM function can help here. TRIM removes any leading and trailing spaces, as well as duplicated spaces inside a text entry.

Insert a new column to the right of AE and make sure it is formatted as General, or else your formula will appear, instead of "Rear" or "Front". Format the column by highlighting it, then clicking the Home tab. Select General from the options in the drop-down list.

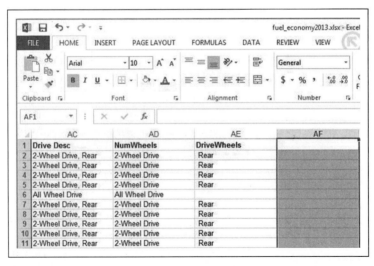

Source: Department of Energy.

Note: New column in fuel efficiency data.

In cell AF2, enter the trim formula: "=TRIM(AE2)". This says, Trim the contents of cell AE2. Hit Enter and you should see the new, trimmed version. Copy this for all of your cells in this column by double-clicking on the square at the bottom right of your cursor box.

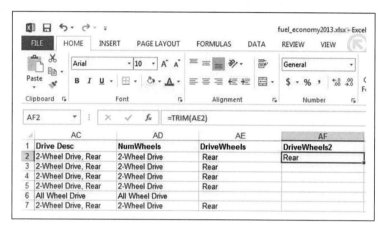

Source: Department of Energy.

Note: Trim function.

These are just two examples of how you can carve data in Excel using Text to Columns. Sometimes we do the opposite and combine the contents of multiple columns into one. For that, we turn to concatenation.

CONCATENATE TO PASTE

We're going to use **concatenation** to put election date data into a proper form. Open the voterturnout.xlsx Excel file, which holds data about voter turnout by precinct in Boone County, Missouri, during the November 2, 2010, general election. The spreadsheet has columns for the precinct or voting district, number of people who voted, number registered and date. All of the dates are recorded as "20101102". Our goal is to turn all of those to 11/2/2010.

We'll use the Text to Columns tool to carve the date and then use concatenation to put the pieces back together. Practice safe computing by copying the contents of Column D into Column E, which we will parse. Highlight E and pick the Text to Columns button from the data menu. That launches a familiar wizard to help. Our data are not delimited this time, so punch the Fixed width button. We can tell that the dates are fixed width because the characters for year, month and day are in consistent locations.

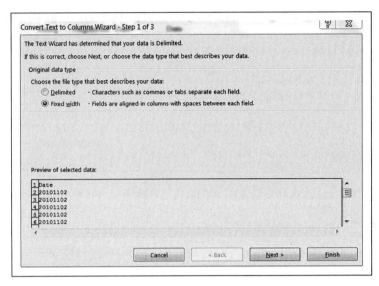

Note: Step 1 in Text to Columns for fixed-width text.

Click Next and we're at Step 2. In this screen, we create the column dividers by clicking where we'd like them to go inside the Data preview area. Don't worry if you put a break in the wrong position—Excel allows you to move or remove it. Create column breaks at positions 4 and 6, just like this.

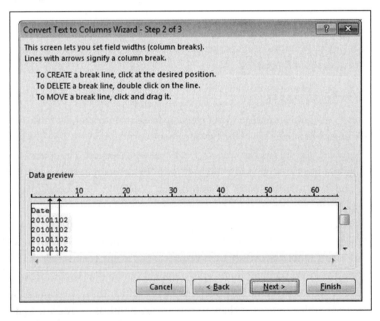

Note: Step 2 in Text to Columns for fixed-width text.

Click Next and go to the final step. Make sure all of the new columns are set to text and click Finish.

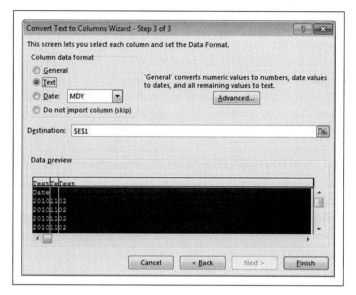

Note: Step 3 in Text to Columns for fixed-width text.

Success! Excel has put the year in Column E, month in F and date in G. Label those three columns accordingly and save a working copy of the file with File | Save as.

	Precinct	Voting	Registered	Date	Date		
1							
2	1A	360	1030	20101102	2010	11	02
3	1B	234	420	20101102	2010	11	02
4	1C	708	1159	20101102	2010	11	02
5	1D	474	1136	20101102	2010	11	02
6	1E	75	2704	20101102	2010	11	02
7	1F	162	1011	20101102	2010	11	02
8	1G	373	759	20101102	2010	11	02
9	1I	163	1026	20101102	2010	11	02
10	2A	629	957	20101102	2010	11	02
11	2B	503	1171	20101102	2010	11	02
12	2C	525	1313	20101102	2010	11	02

Source: Boone County, Missouri, Clerk.

Note: Fixed-width text parsed.

Label Column H as "Date2", which is where we'll put the restructured date that we'll build with concatenation, which uses the ampersand (&) character.

In cell H2 enter "=F2&"/"". This tells Excel to take the contents of cell F2 (or 11 for the month of November) and tack on a slash. We need to put the slash in double quotation marks, so Excel treats it as a text character. We get "11/" for a result, which is a good start.

Next we will tack on the date, by building on the formula "=F2&"/"&G2". Now we see "11/02".

As the last step, will add another slash and the year: "=F2&"/"&G2&"/"&E2". Now we have "11/02/2010" in our cell. Copy this for all of the cells in Column H and format it as a short date. Save the file and close it.

DATE TRICKS

Excel offers other functions that transform data stored in dates. These are handy for generating a month or a year. Open the disaster_declarations.xlsx Excel file and we'll see how this works. This file, originally downloaded from the federal government's Data.gov portal, holds data about more than 4,100 major disasters declared since 1953. Under federal law, state governors may request a declaration of a major disaster and receive federal assistance (Federal Emergency Management Agency, n.d.). In Column G, we have a declaration date, but not a month or year. So it would be difficult if we wanted to analyze the data from either of those dimensions.

Excel's YEAR and MONTH function can extract these data. We'll use another function to generate the day of week, by name, for the declaration dates.

Insert three columns between columns G and H, so we have a place to put the year, month and day of the week. Label these "Year", "Month" and "Day". Format these columns as General.

In cell H4, enter "=Year(G4)" and "1953" appears. Copy this formula for all of the cells.

In cell I4, enter "=Month(G4)" and "5" appears for May. Copy this formula for all of the cells.

In cell J4, enter "=TEXT(A4, "dddd")" and Sunday appears. Copy this formula for all of the cells. The TEXT function, in this case, returns a text value from the data stored in A4. dddd tells Excel to generate the day using its full name. Use ddd to generate an abbreviation.

Use File | Save As to save a working copy of your file and close it.

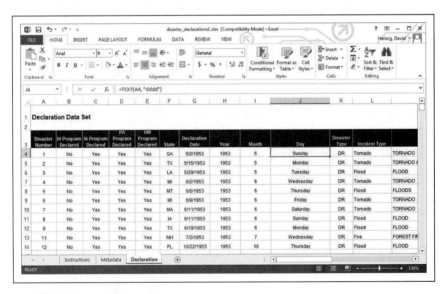

Source: Federal Emergency Management Agency.

Note: Year, month and day extracted from date in Federal Emergency Management Agency disaster declaration data set.

POWER SCRUBBING WITH OPENREFINE

OpenRefine, a free and open-source program, can help for many data cleaning challenges. (Find the program for Windows, Mac and Linux operating systems here: https://github.com/OpenRefine/OpenRefine/wiki/Installation-Instructions.) We'll use OpenRefine to perform one of the most common, frustrating and time-consuming tasks: standardizing data entries. In Chapter 5, we learned how poor data-entry controls can lead to messy data. Such is the case in this Excel file of campaign contributions released by the Missouri Ethics Commission named mo12contribs.xlsx. Open the file and note that we have 19,867 rows, including one for the headers. Each row represents a campaign contribution made by a person, company or political committee. We can take an educated guess that Column J, which has the city of the contributor, might have a lot of typos.

Start OpenRefine. In Windows, the program launches a command-line window, which you might be familiar with if you have ever done any programming. Then it opens the program inside your default browser—here Google Chrome. Note that the address that Chrome is pointed to is http://127.0.0.1:3333, which refers to your machine. In other words, the browser is working locally, not over the Internet.

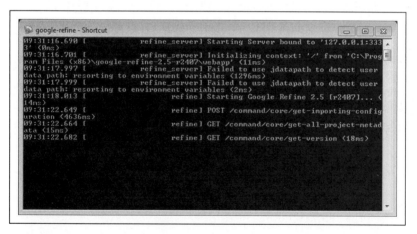

Source: OpenRefine.

Note: OpenRefine command-line window. OpenRefine opens this window upon startup on Windows machines.

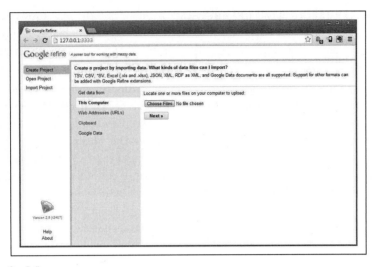

Source: OpenRefine.

Note: OpenRefine create project screen.

Let's create a project in Refine, so we can clean the data. Click Create Project | Get data from | This Computer and find the mo12contribs.xlsx file. Click Next and Refine takes us to the next step for loading the file.

Change the project name to "Campaign contributions" and make sure that the option to parse next line as column header at the bottom is checked. This tells Refine to use the first row from the Excel file as column headers. Note that the top of the screen previews our data.

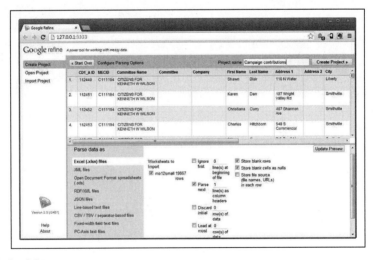

Source: OpenRefine.

Note: OpenRefine project preview screen.

Click Create project and Refine loads the data. By default, it shows only 10 rows at a time. You can change that if you like. Working with data in Refine typically takes two steps: detecting data problems, then correcting them. One of the most common ways to detect the flaws is by creating **Facets**, or views of your data that are very much like spreadsheet pivot tables.

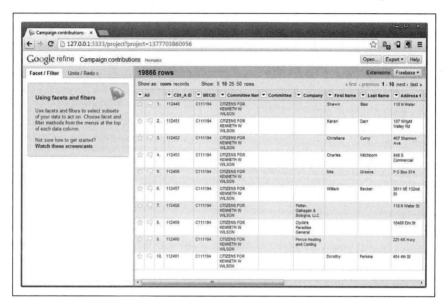

Source: Missouri Ethics Commission.

Note: OpenRefine project screen, data successfully loaded.

Create a Facet for the City column by clicking on its drop-down arrow, then selecting Facet | Text facet from the menu. Scroll down the results and we can see, for example, that the city of St. Louis (proper spelling) has been misspelled many different ways. We could click on the edit line for each misspelling and manually change the city names to our proper spelling, but that would take a whole lot of time. Fortunately, Refine has some powerful tools that will allow us to clean up these misspelled city names en masse.

That's where Clustering can help. **Clustering** uses algorithms designed to detect text values that might be the

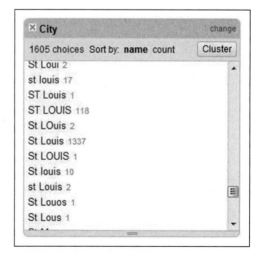

Source: Missouri Ethics Commission.

Note: Text facet for City column. Note that the results are very similar to those created by an Excel pivot table.

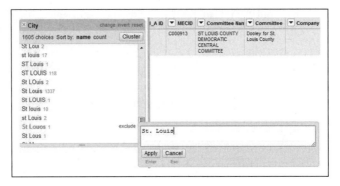

Source: Missouri Ethics Commission.

Note: Manually editing a misspelling.

same. Go ahead and click the Cluster button on the Facet box for City. Refine employs two methods for clustering—key collision and nearest neighbor. Each of those methods has multiple Keying Functions. By default, Refine clusters by key collision/fingerprint. For details about how these algorithms work, see the documentation at https://github.com/OpenRefine/OpenRefine/wiki/Clustering-In-Depth.

Using key collision/fingerprint, Refine shows us how it has clustered city names, including many St. Louis variants at the top of the list. Let's look closely: Refine says the Cluster Size is 13, or that it found 13 different values for clustering here. The Row Count is 2,457. Under Values in Cluster, we see the 13 different spellings. Merge? asks whether we want to transform these values into something else. We do, so check this box. In the New Cell Value box, enter our proper spelling of St. Louis.

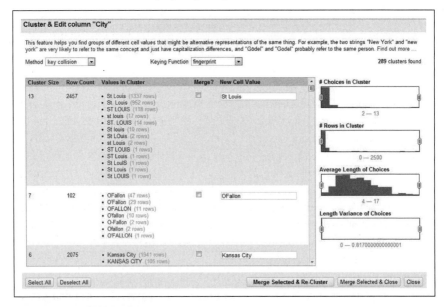

Source: Missouri Ethics Commission.

Note: Clustering in OpenRefine.

Cluster Size	Row Count	Values in Cluster	Merge?	New Cell Value
13	2457	• St Louis (1337 rows) • St. Louis (952 rows) • ST LOUIS (118 rows) • st louis (17 rows) • ST. LOUIS (14 rows) • St louis (10 rows) • St LOuis (2 rows) • st Louis (2 rows) • ST LOUIS (1 rows) • ST Louis (1 rows) • St LouiS (1 rows) • St Louis (1 rows) • St LOUIS (1 rows)	☑	St Louis

Source: Missouri Ethics Commission.

Note: Detail of clustering for variations of St. Louis.

Click Merge Selected & Re-Cluster and Refine **standardizes** all of those St. Louis misspellings. We see that we have a whole bunch more for O'Fallon, Kansas City, Lee's Summit and so on. If we were really using this column for analysis or visualization, we'd want to go through each of these clusters, then apply all of the other methods and keying functions. Close the clustering box.

Let's export our cleaned data as an Excel file by picking Export | Excel at the top right. Refine creates a file in the older (.xls) format that has the same name as our project.

This is just a quick look at how Refine can detect and correct errors. Refine can also split and merge values in columns. It even has its own scripting language called GREL, which allows you to write code for cleaning data.

Close Refine by closing your browser window, then close the window with the command line terminal. If you forget to do the latter, Refine will continue to run in the background.

EXTRACTING DATA FROM PDFS

Let's tackle one last challenge that you might face while gathering data: converting data tables inside PDF files into Excel files. Many government agencies publish data tables trapped inside these PDFs. In order to work with the tables, we must first liberate them. Open the PDF called fy2012_US_gov_net_cost.pdf. This one-page table, which documents the net operating costs of federal agencies, was extracted from the larger Financial Report of the U.S. Government for Fiscal Year 2012 that was released by the Department of the Treasury. We could try copying and pasting the data into Excel, but that would not preserve the column layout. So we'll instead need to use an online converter that will turn the PDF file into an Excel table. Cometdocs (at www.cometdocs.com) and Zamzar (at www.zamzar.com) are two proven services. Sometimes one does better than the other, depending on how the PDF is structured. So try both in real-life situations. (Note that these conversions will not work with PDFs that were created by scanning other documents. You would need to use OCR—or Optical Character Recognition—software to convert those.)

Go to Cometdocs and upload the PDF. Then drag the icon for the uploaded PDF onto the Convert button and pick Excel (xls) from the options list. Enter your email address and click Convert. Now check your email for a message from Cometdocs with the download link.

Open the Excel file and you'll see Cometdocs did a good job converting the PDF. The only glitch is that some agencies, like Health and Human Services, take up more than one line. We could clean that manually in the file if we needed to.

		Gross	Earned		Changes in	Net
9	(Gain)/Loss					
10	from					
11		Gross	Earned		Changes in	Net
12	(In billions of dollars)	Cost	Revenue	Subtotal	Assumptions	Cost
13	Department of Health and Human					
14	Services	924.0	67.8	856.2	0.3	856.5
15	Social Security Administration	825.4	0.3	825.1	-	825.1
16	Department of Defense	784.7	56.0	728.7	70.4	799.1
17	Department of Veterans Affairs	213.6	4.1	209.5	149.3	358.8
18	Interest on Treasury Securities Held by					
19	the Public	245.4	-	245.4	-	245.4
20	Department of Agriculture	161.0	12.0	149.0	-	149.0
21	Office of Personnel Management	48.2	19.1	29.1	98.9	128.0
22	Department of Labor	107.3	-	107.3	-	107.3
23	Department of Transportation	79.0	0.8	78.2	-	78.2
24	Department of Housing and Urban					
25	Development	74.5	1.5	73.0	-	73.0
26	Department of Energy	60.8	4.3	56.5	-	56.5
27	Department of Homeland Security	58.2	9.9	48.3	0.4	48.7
28	Department of Education	62.7	20.0	42.7	-	42.7
29	Department of Justice	38.9	1.3	37.6	-	37.6

Source: Department of the Treasury.

Note: Data extracted from a PDF into an Excel file by Cometdocs.

For students and professionals working with data, cleaning is an essential part of the process. This chapter showed how you can get started to solve some of the most vexing problems with Excel, OpenRefine and online PDF converters.

Now that we know how to check and clean our data, we can move on to analyzing it to discover meaning.

ON YOUR OWN

Use OpenRefine to continue cleaning the campaign contributions data file. Clean the spellings of at least 10 cities. Use all of the algorithms available under clustering. Which one worked the best? Why?

CHAPTER 8 NUMBER SUMMARIES AND COMPARISONS

So far, we have learned how to identify, obtain, evaluate and clean our data. All of this is necessary to get ready for the next step: learning how to analyze our data so we can make better decisions or become more informed. This chapter introduces concepts that can help us develop best practices for analyzing data. Chapters 9 and 10 will show how to use Excel or other spreadsheet programs to generate meaningful information with formulas and pivot tables.

When we work with data, we often generate what are called **summary statistics**. Some examples are counts, sums and averages. These numbers are used to take snapshots or provide descriptions of our data. We can generate these easily and they will tell us much about our data.

This book does not cover how to generate **inferential statistics**, which are used by researchers who have obtained data from a sample and want to use it to draw conclusions about the overall population. For example, researchers would use inferential statistics to predict the outcome of a presidential election based on the responses of 1,000 likely voters. For an overview of inferential statistics, you can read *Seeing Through Statistics* (Utts, 2014) or the IBM *SPSS Statistics Guide to Data Analysis* (Norusis, 2011). Both are easy to understand and take a hands-on approach to learning.

When we work with data, we will often compare numbers, because raw numbers hardly ever are meaningful by themselves. We create meaning when we compare them to other numbers or benchmarks. Let's explore this concept by considering how much money the U.S. government spent in fiscal year 2012 on national defense programs (Financial Management Service, 2013).

The federal government spent more than $680.4 billion on this category, which includes homeland security. Sounds like a pretty huge number, right? Maybe not so much when you compare it to the amount the U.S. government spent in the previous fiscal year (2011): more than $708.2 billion. Subtract those numbers and we see that spending for defense actually decreased by around $27.8 billion. How significant of a change was that for defense? Calculate the percent change and you get a 3.9 percent decrease. By comparing numbers over time, we can generate some information that's interesting and meaningful.

We can do the same by comparing defense spending to other categories. How does fiscal year 2012 spending on national defense stack up to spending on Social Security, the federal program that guarantees income to retirees, survivors of deceased workers and disabled workers? In fiscal year 2012, the federal government spent more than $773.2 billion on Social Security. Compare that to the $680.4 billion in defense spending and you will see that it was $92.8 billion—or 13.6 percent—more.

How significant, respectively, are defense and Social Security in terms of all spending by the U.S. government? To calculate that we will need to compare each individual amount to the more than $3.5 trillion in total outlays for 2012 to generate a percent of total. Social Security accounts for the largest share, at around 21.9 percent, or a little more than one fifth. Defense spending accounts for around 19.2 percent, or a little less than one fifth.

SIMPLE SUMMARY STATISTICS

We'll start with the simplest kinds of numbers that we can generate from our data: summary statistics. Summary statistics are very useful because they can tell us a lot about our data. However, summary statistics can sometimes be misleading, as we shall see.

Count tells us how many items we have in our data. It helps us to answer questions that start with, "How many . . . ?" In our spreadsheets, we can count data stored as numbers, text and dates.

Sum gives us the total amount for all items in our data. For instance, we could sum the total number of people who were registered to vote, as noted in our voter turnout spreadsheet file. Sum helps us answer questions that start with, "How much . . . ?" Sum only works with data stored as numbers.

Averages generate what statisticians call the **central tendency**, or a number that best represents a collection of numbers. Averages only work with data stored as numbers.

Using averages can get tricky, because we have three measures at our disposal: the mean, the median and the mode. The **mean** is the arithmetic average, the number that's generated by adding our numbers and then dividing by the number of cases. This is probably the first average you learned in elementary school. So, if we have the three numbers 1, 2 and 3, we would add them for a sum of 6, then divide by the number of cases (3) to get our average of 2.

The **median** is the midpoint in a set of numbers, ordered from low to high. So our median for the same numbers would be 2. If we have an even number of numbers, spreadsheets calculate the median by running the mean on the two numbers in the middle. So the median for 1, 3, 5 and 7 would be 4 (3+5/2). As you can see, a median can be a little confusing at first, because it might be a number that does not appear in a data set.

Outliers, or numbers that are notably low or high, can skew the mean. In those instances, the median is a more accurate reflection of the central tendency. Numbers with an unlimited cap—such as incomes or home sale prices—are more prone to having outliers. Major League baseball player salary data provide a great example. Players like the Los

Angeles Dodgers' Zack Greinke, who are at the top of the chart with tens of millions of dollars in annual pay, help push the mean way above the median.

The **mode** is the number that appears most frequently in a data set. Our mode for 1, 2, 2, 5, 7, and 12 would be 2. In this case, the mean (4.8) and median (3.8) are more representative of the central tendency than the mode. In truth, we will rarely use the mode to generate summary statistics. We will use mean and median instead.

Two other useful summary statistics can help us determine the range of values that we have for spreadsheet data that are stored as numbers or dates. The minimum is the smallest number or earliest date in our data. The maximum is the largest number or most recent date in our data.

COMPARED TO WHAT?

The challenge we face when analyzing data is in making our results meaningful to ourselves and to others. Whenever we have a raw number, it derives meaning from its relationship to other numbers. So we always want to ask, Compared to what? Fortunately, we have in our analytical toolbox a number of comparisons that are easy to generate using spreadsheet programs. They are amount change or raw change, percent change, percent of total, ratios and rates. We'll consider each of these using the federal outlays data from the introduction in this chapter.

We see from the outlays report available online as a PDF at http://www.fiscal.treasury .gov/fsreports/rpt/combStmt/cs2012/outlay.pdf that the federal government spent more than $14.7 billion on energy-related items in fiscal year 2012. That sounds like a whole lot of money, certainly more than any of us will amass in our lifetimes.

However, we have no way of knowing just how significant this amount is, because we haven't put it into context. Let's compare the amount for 2012 to the amount for 2011, which was more than $12.0 billion. So to calculate the **amount change** or **raw change** we subtract the amount from 2011 from the amount from 2012 and get a result of roughly $2.7 billion.

A $2.7 billion increase sounds like a big boost for U.S. government spending on energy. We can show just how big of an increase that is by comparing it to our starting point of 2011. This generates the **percent change**. To calculate that, divide the amount change by the starting point. So we would divide $2.7 billion by $12.0 billion and get a result of roughly 22.2 percent.

Of course, we should calculate the amount and percent change for all of our spending categories to get results that we could compare to those amounts for energy.

Let's go back to the $14.7 billion spent in fiscal year 2012. We can compare that amount to the total spent by the U.S. government that year to calculate the **percent of total**. So divide $14.7 billion by more than $3.53 trillion to get just more than four-tenths of 1 percent. So spending on energy was just a sliver of the total pie in 2012. National defense, in contrast, took up nearly one fifth (or around 19.2 percent) of the total.

Ratios also can help us understand relationships between numbers. Ratios are helpful when we want to calculate proportions that show differences between numbers. To generate a ratio we take our number and divide it by another number to which we are drawing a comparison. For example, the average pay gap between U.S. chief executive officers at publicly traded corporations was 204:1 (Smith, 2013). In other words, for every $1 earned by a worker, the chief executive earned $204. In education, we often hear about student-to-teacher ratios; they can help us determine if classrooms are overcrowded. With our federal spending data we can compare defense to energy spending to get a defense-to-energy ratio. Divide the $680.4 billion for defense spending by the $14.7 billion for energy and we get a 46:1 ratio. So for every $1 the government spent on energy, it spent $46 on defense.

Finally, **rates** are helpful tools because they allow us to more fairly compare numbers from areas with dissimilar populations. Rates helped *The New York Times* show that small cities like Rehoboth Beach in Delaware and Palm Springs in California had displaced San Francisco and West Hollywood as strongholds for households headed by same-sex couples (Tavernise, 2011). The newspaper calculated rates of same-sex couples per 1,000 households, using data from decennial censuses.

Usually when we generate rates we first calculate a per capita—or per person— number. Then we multiply that by a standard number to normalize our results.

The New York Times compared the same-sex couple population numbers to the total number of households in each city for its analysis. To do that, it divided the same-sex couples by the total number of households.

After generating a per household rate, it multiplied that rate by 1,000 so it could express the number in terms of 1,000 households. Per capita rates are usually so small that they are fractions of numbers and don't make much sense. So we normally multiply them by a standard number, which is something the data source can provide. Crime rates based on the FBI's Uniform Crime Reporting System data are typically calculated per 100,000 people. Medical and health-care statistics often are expressed in terms of 100,000 people.

BENCHMARKING

Another way to think about number comparisons is by thinking about **benchmarks**. We can have internal and external benchmarks. Internal benchmarks are numbers that are contained within our data. For example, our ratio of 2012 defense to energy spending could be considered an internal benchmark because we are comparing two amounts from the same year. Percent change could be considered an external benchmark because we are comparing a number from one year to that number in the previous year. Reports created by government agencies, or nongovernmental organizations using data, can be a benchmarking tool. These reports often will contain summary statistics or other figures that we can compare to our own data.

Now that we've seen how we can use summary statistics and number comparisons to generate meaning from our data, we're going to learn how to calculate summary statistics and number comparisons using Excel in the next two chapters.

ON YOUR OWN

Download the 2011UScrime.xls from the book website and then open it. Inspect the file and see that it contains data about crimes as reported by U.S. cities to the FBI, along with populations. Name and explain three number comparisons that you could make to generate some meaningful statistics.

CHAPTER 9 CALCULATING SUMMARY STATISTICS AND NUMBER COMPARISONS

N ow that you know how summary statistics and number comparisons can help you find meaning inside data, it's time to use Excel to run these calculations. We're going to work with a file called city_crime.xlsx from the book website for our analysis in this chapter. In the next chapter, we'll learn how to use Excel to sort, filter and group and summarize our data.

Open the file and examine it. You'll see that we have 2011 and 2012 population, violent crime and property crime data for 31 U.S. cities with 2012 populations greater than 500,000. Chicago and Tucson are missing because their crime data were incomplete.

	A	B	C	D	E	F	G	H
1	State	City	Population 2011	Violent crime 2011	Property crime 2011	Population 2012	Violent crime 2012	Property crime 2012
2	NEW YORK	New York	8,211,875	51,209	140,457	8,289,415	52,993	142,760
3	CALIFORNIA	Los Angeles	3,837,207	20,045	86,330	3,855,122	18,547	87,478
4	TEXAS	Houston	2,143,628	20,892	108,336	2,177,273	21,610	107,678
5	PENNSYLVANIA	Philadelphia	1,530,873	18,268	59,617	1,538,957	17,853	56,997
6	ARIZONA	Phoenix	1,466,097	8,089	64,479	1,485,509	9,458	60,777
7	NEVADA	Las Vegas Metropolitan Police Department	1,458,474	10,813	41,426	1,479,393	11,598	46,427
8	TEXAS	San Antonio	1,355,339	7,038	80,868	1,380,123	6,943	82,668
9	CALIFORNIA	San Diego	1,316,919	5,104	29,709	1,338,477	5,529	31,700
10	TEXAS	Dallas	1,223,021	8,330	61,859	1,241,549	8,380	54,300
11	CALIFORNIA	San Jose	957,062	3,206	21,972	976,459	3,547	28,463
12	FLORIDA	Jacksonville	834,429	5,182	36,113	840,660	5,189	34,674
13	INDIANA	Indianapolis	833,024	9,170	46,967	838,650	9,942	46,898
14	TEXAS	Austin	807,022	3,471	42,250	832,901	3,405	43,472
15	CALIFORNIA	San Francisco	814,701	5,374	32,886	820,363	5,777	38,898
16	NORTH CAROLINA	Charlotte-Mecklenburg	789,478	4,787	32,008	808,504	5,238	32,587

Source: Federal Bureau of Investigation.

Note: Uniform Crime Report data from the FBI, open in Excel.

The author created this spreadsheet using separate 2011 and 2012 FBI Uniform Crime Report Excel files that he downloaded from the bureau's annual Crime in the United States reports at http://www.fbi.gov/about-us/cjis/ucr/ucr-publications#Crime. The FBI provides data about eight major crimes: murder or non-negligent manslaughter, forcible rape, robbery and aggravated assault all are categorized as violent crimes; burglary, larceny-theft, motor vehicle theft and arson are categorized as property crimes.

Using the concepts we learned in Chapter 8, we are going to analyze this spreadsheet to generate some meaningful information

SUM CRIMES BY YEAR

As a first step, let's calculate total crime for each year in each city. In Cell I1 type "Total crime 2011" for a column header and hit Enter. Type "Total crime 2012" in J1 for a column header.

In Cell I2, calculate New York City's total crime for 2011 by entering this formula: "=E2+D2". All Excel formulas start with the = sign and use **cell references** as much as possible. This tells Excel to add the value in D2 (the violent crimes for New York City in 2011) to the value in E2 (the property crimes for New York City in 2011). You should get 191,666 for your result. (Note: We can also subtract (–), divide (/) and multiply (*) in Excel.)

Copy this formula for 2011 crime down for all of the other cities by putting the cursor block in cell I2 and double-clicking on the block at the bottom right corner. (You could also drag this handle down until you get to cell I32 for Fresno.) Even though numbers appear for the cities' 2011 total crimes, our cells really contain formulas. We can check this out by clicking into cell I3 for Los Angeles. Excel's formula bar tells us that "=D3+E3" is what the cell contains. Notice that Excel was smart enough to adjust the formula by increasing the row number in each cell reference by one.

	B	C	D	E	F	G	H	I	J
I3				=D3+E3					
	City	Population 2011	Violent crime 2011	Property crime 2011	Population 2012	Violent crime 2012	Property crime 2012	Total crime 2011	Total crime 2012
2	New York	8,211,875	51,209	140,457	8,289,415	52,993	142,760	191,666	
3	Los Angeles	3,837,207	20,045	86,330	3,855,122	18,547	87,478	106,375	
4	Houston	2,143,628	20,892	108,336	2,177,273	21,610	107,678	129,228	
5	Philadelphia	1,530,873	18,268	59,617	1,538,957	17,853	56,997	77,885	
6	Phoenix	1,466,097	8,089	64,479	1,485,509	9,458	60,777	72,568	
7	Las Vegas Metropolitan Police Department	1,458,474	10,813	41,426	1,479,393	11,598	46,427	52,239	
8	San Antonio	1,355,339	7,038	80,868	1,380,123	6,943	82,668	87,906	
9	San Diego	1,316,919	5,104	29,709	1,338,477	5,529	31,700	34,813	
10	Dallas	1,223,021	8,330	61,859	1,241,549	8,380	54,300	70,189	

Source: Federal Bureau of Investigation.

Note: Calculating total crimes for cities.

Now enter in J2 the formula to calculate total crimes for New York City in 2012 (195,753): "=G2+H2". Copy that down for all of the other cities.

Practice safe computing by saving a working copy of the file using File | Save As, using a new file name.

MINIMUM AND MAXIMUM NUMBERS

It would be good for us to know the range of numbers in each of our eight columns. Let's do that at the bottom of the sheet. Scroll down to Cell B34 and enter "Minimum". Below it, in Cell B35, enter "Maximum". To calculate the minimum of the 2011 population enter this formula in Cell C34: "=MIN(C2:C32)". This tells Excel to calculate the minimum number (500,480) for all cells from C2 through C32. Copy that formula for all of the other cells by dragging the handle at the bottom right of the cursor.

To get the maximum of each column, enter this into Cell 35: "=MAX(C2:C32)" and copy it to the right. This generates some interesting data, such as the range of violent crime reports in 2011—2,858 to 51,209.

AMOUNT CHANGE

If we were analyzing these data for year-over-year trends we would want to know how much crime changed in each of our cities. We'll calculate the amount change. First enter "VC change" in Cell K1, "PC change" in Cell L1 and "Total crime change" in Cell M1.

Now we will calculate amount change, starting with the violent crime change in Cell K2. Enter "=G2–D2" to subtract the 2011 violent crimes for New York City from the 2012 violent crimes. We see an increase of 1,784. Copy the formula down for all of the cities and see that some of them, including Los Angeles, experienced decreases in the number of violent crimes reported.

To calculate the amount change for property crimes in cell L2, enter "=H2–E2" and copy it for all. Likewise, calculate the amount change for all crimes in cell M2 by entering "=J2–I2" and copying for all of the cities.

Your spreadsheet should look something like this:

	A	B	I	J	K	L	M
1	State	City	Total crime 2011	Total crime 2012	VC change	PC change	Total crime change
2	NEW YORK	New York	191,666	195,753	1,784	2,303	4,087
3	CALIFORNIA	Los Angeles	106,375	106,025	-1,498	1,148	-350
4	TEXAS	Houston	129,228	129,288	718	-658	60
5	PENNSYLVANIA	Philadelphia	77,885	74,850	-415	-2,620	-3,035
6	ARIZONA	Phoenix	72,568	70,235	1,369	-3,702	-2,333
7	NEVADA	Las Vegas Metropolitan Police Department	52,239	58,025	785	5,001	5,786
8	TEXAS	San Antonio	87,906	89,611	-95	1,800	1,705
9	CALIFORNIA	San Diego	34,813	37,229	425	1,991	2,416
10	TEXAS	Dallas	70,189	62,680	50	-7,559	-7,509

Source: Federal Bureau of Investigation.

Note: Calculating amount change in Excel.

STEPPING UP TO PERCENT CHANGE

To reinforce the concept from the last chapter, the amount (or raw) change doesn't say much, because we lack context. That's why we always want to compare the raw change to original numbers to generate the percent change. We'll use columns N, O and P for those calculations. So enter "VC % change", "PC % change" and "Total crime % change" as headers in Row 1 of those columns.

For each column we will need to compare the amount change to the starting points in 2011 by dividing. To calculate the percent change in violent crime, enter this in cell

N2: "=K2/D2". This divides the change by the number of violent crimes in 2011. Excel returns less than a whole number: .03484. Excel is expressing percent in terms of the number 1, because the column is formatted as general, not percentage. Soon, we will format the column as percentages, so we will see that the increase really is just shy of 3.5 percent.

In O2, enter this formula to calculate the percent change for property crimes: "=L2/E2". This divides the amount change by the number in 2011. In P2, enter "=M2/I2" to divide the change in total crimes by the number in 2011. Copy the formulas down for columns N, O and P.

It's difficult to distinguish between our numbers because Excel is reporting them as decimals. We will change the formatting so they appear as percentages instead. Select Columns N through P, then right-click on any of the header letters. Select the Format Cells . . . option from the popup menu and the cell formatting box opens.

Source: Microsoft Excel for Windows 2013.

Note: Percent change column currently set to General.

Under the Number tab, pick Percentage as the Category. Set the number of decimal places to 1 and click OK to make the changes.

Source: Microsoft Excel for Windows 2013.

Note: Setting percent change column to Percentage with 1 decimal place.

Now we can see that the data in our percent change columns really do look like percentages. Save your work.

	A	B	N	O	P
			VC %	PC %	Total crime %
1	State	City	change	change	change
2	NEW YORK	New York	3.5%	1.6%	2.1%
3	CALIFORNIA	Los Angeles	-7.5%	1.3%	-0.3%
4	TEXAS	Houston	3.4%	-0.6%	0.0%
5	PENNSYLVANIA	Philadelphia	-2.3%	-4.4%	-3.9%
6	ARIZONA	Phoenix	16.9%	-5.7%	-3.2%
7	NEVADA	Las Vegas Metropolitan Police Department	7.3%	12.1%	11.1%
8	TEXAS	San Antonio	-1.3%	2.2%	1.9%
9	CALIFORNIA	San Diego	8.3%	6.7%	6.9%
10	TEXAS	Dallas	0.6%	-12.2%	-10.7%
11	CALIFORNIA	San Jose	10.6%	29.5%	27.1%

Source: Federal Bureau of Investigation.

Note: Percent change columns properly formatted.

RUNNING RATES

Now we're ready to generate some more-meaningful information by calculating crime rates. Rates allow us to more fairly compare areas that have different populations, such as New York City (more than 8.2 million) to Fresno (just a bit greater than 500,000).

When we calculate rates, it's a two-step process. First, we calculate a per person, or per capita, rate. Then, we calculate the rate per a set number of people. Here's where we'll use the FBI's standard of 100,000 people. We should calculate these rates for both years, but we will stick to 2012, the most recent in our data file, for this lesson. Use Columns Q–V and enter these as headers in Row 1: "2012 VC per Cap", "2012 PC per cap", "2012 Total crime per cap", "2012 VC per 100k", "2012 PC per 100k" and "2012 Total crime per 100k".

In Q2 we will compare the number of violent crimes in 2012 to the population in the same year. The formula is "=G2/F2". Enter and copy it for all of the cities. We get .00639 for New York City, meaning not even one for every person. That number makes no sense, so we will later multiply it by 100,000.

In R2, compare 2012 property crimes to population with this formula: "=H2/F2" and copy it for all of the cities. In S2 compare total crimes for 2012 to population with the formula "=J2/F2" and copy it for all the cities as well. Your spreadsheet should look like this:

	A	B	Q	R	S	T	U	V
1	State	City	2012 VC per cap	2012 PC per cap	2012 Total crime per cap	2012 VC per 100k	2012 PC per 100k	2012 Total crime per 100k
2	NEW YORK	New York	0.00639	0.01722	0.02361			
3	CALIFORNIA	Los Angeles	0.00481	0.02269	0.0275			
4	TEXAS	Houston	0.00993	0.04946	0.05938			
5	PENNSYLVANIA	Philadelphia	0.0116	0.03704	0.04864			
6	ARIZONA	Phoenix	0.00637	0.04091	0.04728			
7	NEVADA	Las Vegas Metropolitan Police Department	0.00784	0.03138	0.03922			
8	TEXAS	San Antonio	0.00503	0.0599	0.06493			
9	CALIFORNIA	San Diego	0.00413	0.02368	0.02781			
10	TEXAS	Dallas	0.00675	0.04374	0.05049			
11	CALIFORNIA	San Jose	0.00363	0.02915	0.03278			
12	FLORIDA	Jacksonville	0.00617	0.04125	0.04742			

Source: Federal Bureau of Investigation.

Note: Per capita crime rates.

Now, we're ready to calculate rates per 100,000 population. In T2 for New York City, enter "=Q2*100000" to multiply the per person violent crime rate by our standard. Much better! Excel tells us that the rate is more than 639 violent crimes for every 100,000 people. Copy that down for the rest of the cities.

Calculate the other rates per 100,000 people by entering the following formula for the property crime rate in U2: "=R2*100000". Then, enter in V2 "=S2*100000" for the total crime rate per 100,000. Note that each city's total crime rate per 100,000 is the sum of its property and violent crime rates. Our results have an inconsistent number of decimal places because our columns are formatted as general. Using the Format Cells options, change Columns T–V to Number with one decimal place. Save your work. Your spreadsheet should look like this:

	A	B	T	U	V
					2012 Total crime
			2012 VC	2012 PC	crime
1	State	City	per 100k	per 100k	per 100k
2	NEW YORK	New York	639.3	1722.2	2361.5
3	CALIFORNIA	Los Angeles	481.1	2269.1	2750.2
4	TEXAS	Houston	992.5	4945.5	5938.1
5	PENNSYLVANIA	Philadelphia	1160.1	3703.6	4863.7
6	ARIZONA	Phoenix	636.7	4091.3	4728.0
7	NEVADA	Las Vegas Metropolitan Police Department	784.0	3138.2	3922.2
8	TEXAS	San Antonio	503.1	5989.9	6493.0
9	CALIFORNIA	San Diego	413.1	2368.4	2781.4
10	TEXAS	Dallas	675.0	4373.6	5048.5
11	CALIFORNIA	San Jose	363.3	2914.9	3278.2

Source: Federal Bureau of Investigation.

Note: Crime rates per 100,000 population.

Eyeball the results for the violent crime rate per 100,000 and it looks like New York City is in the middle of the pack. We'll figure that out for sure in the next chapter, when we learn how to sort our results. (Note: We could calculate per 100,000 person crime rates in one step using a formula like this: =crime number/population*100000.)

RUNNING RATIOS

We can use ratios in our analysis here to compare the numbers of property to violent crimes in each city. This could generate some interesting information by showing us in which cities property crimes are more prevalent. To do that, we will need to divide property crimes by violent crimes for each year in Columns W and X. Enter "2011 ratio" and "2012 ratio" into the headers in Row 1.

In W2, we will compare 2011 property to violent crime, so enter "=E2/D2" and copy that for all of the cities. In X2, we will compare the 2012 figures using "=H2/G2". Again, our numbers are not properly formatted, so change them to numbers with one decimal place.

	A	B	W	X
1	**State**	**City**	**2011 ratio**	**2012 ratio**
2	NEW YORK	New York	2.7	2.7
3	CALIFORNIA	Los Angeles	4.3	4.7
4	TEXAS	Houston	5.2	5.0
5	PENNSYLVANIA	Philadelphia	3.3	3.2
6	ARIZONA	Phoenix	8.0	6.4
7	NEVADA	Las Vegas Metropolitan Police Department	3.8	4.0
8	TEXAS	San Antonio	11.5	11.9
9	CALIFORNIA	San Diego	5.8	5.7
10	TEXAS	Dallas	7.4	6.5

Source: Federal Bureau of Investigation.

Note: Ratios of property to violent crimes.

New York City had 2.7 property crimes for every violent crime in 2012. In San Antonio, property crimes were far more prevalent: nearly 12 for every instance of violent crime.

PERCENT OF TOTAL

Another way to check on the prevalence of violent crime in each city is to compare violent crimes to overall crime. We'll do this by calculating the percent of all crimes that are violent.

Use "2011 % violent" and "2012 % violent" for the headers in Columns Y and Z. In Y2, calculate the percentage of crime that was violent in 2011 with this formula: "=D2/I2". Likewise, for 2012 enter "=G2/J2" in Z2. Copy the formulas for all the cities and format the cells as a number with one decimal place.

	A	B	W	X	Y	Z
1	**State**	**City**	**2011 ratio**	**2012 ratio**	**2011 % violent**	**2012 % violent**
2	NEW YORK	New York	2.7	2.7	26.7%	27.1%
3	CALIFORNIA	Los Angeles	4.3	4.7	18.8%	17.5%
4	TEXAS	Houston	5.2	5.0	16.2%	16.7%
5	PENNSYLVANIA	Philadelphia	3.3	3.2	23.5%	23.9%
6	ARIZONA	Phoenix	8.0	6.4	11.1%	13.5%
7	NEVADA	Las Vegas Metropolitan Police Department	3.8	4.0	20.7%	20.0%
8	TEXAS	San Antonio	11.5	11.9	8.0%	7.7%
9	CALIFORNIA	San Diego	5.8	5.7	14.7%	14.9%

Source: Federal Bureau of Investigation.

Note: Violent crime percent of total calculations.

The results support our earlier observation: New York has a much larger proportion of violent crime (27 percent) than San Antonio (7.7 percent).

Save the spreadsheet and close it. We'll use it again in the next chapter.

MORE SUMMARIZING

Before we move on to the next chapter, where we'll learn how to manipulate our data even more, we'll learn a couple more tricks using Excel summary functions. Open the modified 2013_White_House_Staff.xlsx workbook, which was downloaded from the White House website at http://www.whitehouse.gov/21stcenturygov/tools/salaries. Under law, presidential administrations are required to report staff salary data to Congress every year. The spreadsheet holds data about 460 staff members, including their names, positions and salaries. We are going to calculate some basic summary statistics using these data.

Go to the end of the sheet and type some labels: type "Total pay" in B463, "Mean pay" in B464, and "Median pay" in B465. Next, calculate the sum and the two averages next to the labels.

In C463 enter the SUM function: "=SUM(C2:C461)". This sums all of the numbers in that cell range. In C464 enter the formula for the mean: "=AVERAGE(C2:C461)". In C465 enter the formula for the median: "=MEDIAN(C2:C461)". Format those cells as currency with no decimal places and we see the results at left.

Total pay	$37,859,780
Mean pay	$82,304
Median pay	$70,000

Source: Federal Bureau of Investigation.

Note: Calculating summary statistics.

This tells us the staff earned more than $37.8 million. The mean salary was more than $82,000, while the median was $70,000. Those are pretty close, so we can say that these salaries aren't skewed high, as Major League baseball player salaries are.

Use File | Save As to save a working copy of your file.

In this chapter you learned how to use Excel to generate number comparisons that are meaningful. In the next chapter, you will learn how to sort the data to find large numbers and interesting patterns. You will also learn how to filter data and use pivot tables to create summaries for categories in your data.

ON YOUR OWN

Download the comparisons.xlsx file from the book website and follow the directions on each of the three worksheets.

CHAPTER 10

SPREADSHEETS AS DATABASE MANAGERS

S o far, we have used Excel to perform simple spreadsheet operations: doing math, running functions. That has helped us travel far toward our goal of going from data to knowledge. Our next step is learning how to use Excel as a lightweight database manager. We can use Excel to sort and filter our data so we can uncover meaningful patterns. We can use Excel pivot tables to group our data by categories and then calculate summaries (counts, sums and averages) for those groups.

SORTING

Excel and other spreadsheets allow us to sort our data in different ways. We can sort numbers and dates in ascending order, meaning lowest to highest, or alphabetically with text. If we have any negative numbers, those would be listed first because they have a value lower than 0 or any positive numbers. We're going to learn how to sort using our city_crime.xlsx spreadsheet, so open that. We can use sorting to answer questions like, Which city had the highest increase in property crimes? Which city had the lowest violent crime rate in 2012? Which city had the greatest ratio of property to violent crimes in 2012?

Sorting in Excel can be tricky because you first need to highlight all of the data you want to sort, including the headers but excluding any summary functions calculated at the bottom of the sheet. If you fail to highlight all of your data, Excel may sort some of your columns and leave others unsorted. This is a big problem, because you'll have mismatched data. (Note: You can always undo a bad sort by using Ctrl-Z on your keyboard, or the Undo button.)

So we will practice safe computing by first highlighting the data we need to sort. On a PC, put the cursor inside any of the cells containing data or headers. Then, hold down Ctrl-Shift-8 and Excel selects all of your data. Scroll down and see that the rows used to calculate the minimum and maximum are unselected, which is how it should be. Mac users can highlight the block of data using the Command-A key combination.

Now we are ready to sort and discover which city had the lowest violent crime rate in 2012. Select the Data tab and then the big Sort button.

Source: Microsoft Excel for Windows 2013.

Note: Excel sort button.

This opens the Sort dialog box, where we can set the options for sorting. Note that the check box in the upper right should be checked, because our Excel sheet does have header rows (the labels that we created in Chapter 9).

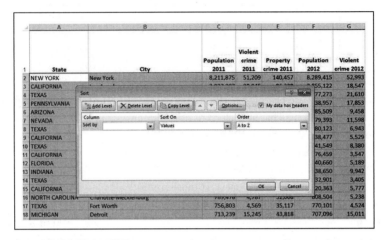

Source: Microsoft Excel for Windows 2013.

Note: Excel sort dialog box.

In the options, Sort by 2012 VC per 100k, Sort On Values and Order Smallest to Largest. The dialog box should look like this:

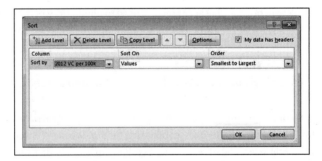

Source: Microsoft Excel for Windows 2013.

Note: Sort by 2012 violent crime per 100,000 population column.

Click OK to sort and we see in Column T that San Jose had the lowest property crime rate in 2012, at 363.3. Austin is second lowest with 408.8.

	A	B	T	U
	State	City	2012 VC per 100k	2012 PC per 100k
2	CALIFORNIA	San Jose	363.3	2914.9
3	TEXAS	Austin	408.8	5219.3
4	CALIFORNIA	San Diego	413.1	2368.4
5	TEXAS	El Paso	423.2	2429.3
6	CALIFORNIA	Los Angeles	481.1	2269.1
7	TEXAS	San Antonio	503.1	5989.9
8	OREGON	Portland	517.2	5092.3
9	CALIFORNIA	Fresno	543.1	5086.3
10	TEXAS	Fort Worth	587.5	4222.0
11	WASHINGTON	Seattle	597.6	5093.8
12	KENTUCKY	Louisville Metro	598.8	4293.9

Source: Federal Bureau of Investigation.

Note: Data sorted ascending by 2012 violent crime rate per 100,000 people.

Let's sort the data again to figure out which city had the highest total crime rate in 2012. If your data block somehow became unselected, select it again using Ctrl-Shift-8. Select the big sort button again and make sure that the My data has headers option is checked.

Then, set Sort by to 2012 Total crime per 100k, Sort on to Values, and Order Largest to Smallest. Select OK and look at the rates in Column V. Memphis is tops with 8,063.1, followed by Detroit at 7,915.0.

	A	B	V
	State	City	2012 Total crime per 100k
2	TENNESSEE	Memphis	8063.1
3	MICHIGAN	Detroit	7915.0
4	OKLAHOMA	Oklahoma City	6860.9
5	INDIANA	Indianapolis	6777.6
6	TEXAS	San Antonio	6493.0
7	WISCONSIN	Milwaukee	6337.6
8	NEW MEXICO	Albuquerque	6117.0
9	MARYLAND	Baltimore	6065.5

Source: Federal Bureau of Investigation.

Note: Total crime rate sorted descending.

We can also sort using more than one column. Let's learn how to do that by sorting our data first by state and then by city. We will see the states listed alphabetically. If any states have more than one city, we'll see those listed alphabetically within the states.

Make sure your data are highlighted and then select the Sort button. Sort by State, Sort on Values and Order A to Z. Then select the Add Level button so we can sort by city next. Set the Then by option to City, Sort on Values and Order A to Z.

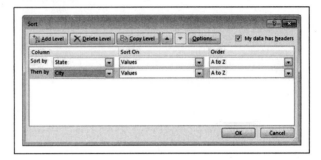

Source: Microsoft Excel for Windows 2013.

Note: Sorting by two columns.

Click OK and we have our alphabetical sort, first by state and then by city. Note that California has more than one city, with Los Angeles at the top and San Jose at the bottom. Save your file. You'll see that it's saved with our state and city sort order. Now close the file.

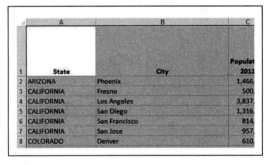

Source: Federal Bureau of Investigation.

Note: Data sorted by state and city.

FILTERING

Another database function that's built into Excel and other spreadsheets is filtering. It allows us to display only those rows of data that meet certain criteria. We will give it a try using the modified 2013_White_House_Staff.xlsx spreadsheet that we worked with in Chapter 9. Look in Column B of the spreadsheet, which lists the status of the employee. Most of these statuses are Employee. But some others say Detailee, to denote employees of other federal agencies who have been temporarily detailed to work in the White House under the Office of Management and Budget's Regulatory Exchange and Training Program. We'll use a filter to show only those who have been detailed to the White House, then show those earning at least $100,000.

Filter

Source: Microsoft Excel for Windows 2013.

Note: Excel filter button.

First, we need to put our cursor inside the block of data that we'd like to filter. Select the Data tab and then the big Filter button, which looks like a funnel.

Drop-down arrows now appear next to each of our columns. These are the controls that we use to filter the data.

	A	B	C	D	E
1	Name	Status	Salary	Pay Basis	Position Title
2	Aberger, Marie E.	Employee	$42000.00	Per Annum	PRESS ASSISTANT
3	Abraham, Yohannes A.	Employee	$120000.00	Per Annum	SPECIAL ASSISTANT TO THE PRESIDENT AND
4	Adler, Caroline E.	Employee	$75000.00	Per Annum	DEPUTY COMMUNICATIONS DIRECTOR
5	Agnew, David P.	Employee	$153500.00	Per Annum	DEPUTY ASSISTANT TO THE PRESIDENT AND I
6	Aguilar, Rita C.	Employee	$90000.00	Per Annum	SENIOR CONFIRMATIONS ADVISOR

Source: The White House.

Note: Drop-down arrows for filters.

Click on the drop-down arrow for Column B and then select only Detailee from the list at the bottom of the box. Click OK and we now see only the people who have been temporarily detailed to the White House.

	A	B
1	Name	Status
19	Baker, Lamar W.	Detailee
30	Berrigan, Elizabeth D.	Detailee
39	Brandt, Kate E.	Detailee
51	Calderon, Tovah R.	Detailee
64	Clark, Melanca D.	Detailee
86	Dawe, Christopher J.	Detailee
106	Elliott, Brandace N.	Detailee
111	Fazili, Sameera	Detailee
114	Ferrell, Taylor N.	Detailee
119	Flores, Andrea R.	Detailee
149	Gunja, Mushtaq Z.	Detailee
186	Johnson, Guy A.	Detailee
224	Lee, Marisa R.	Detailee
230	Leonard, Shelley D.	Detailee
251	Marquez, Laura R.	Detailee
270	McQuaid, Nicholas L.	Detailee

Source: The White House.

Note: Data filtered by Detailee in the Status column.

Note: Excel status bar. The status bar shows how many records have been filtered.

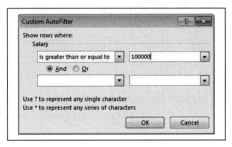

Source: Microsoft Excel for Windows 2013.

Note: Filtering for detailee records where the salary is $100,000 or more.

We have a few clues that our rows are filtered: A funnel appears next to the Status label in B1. The row numbers turn blue. The unfiltered row numbers disappear. And the status bar at the bottom right tells us "28 out of 460 records found". All of our other records still are there, but they're just hidden behind the filter for now.

Now we are going to filter to show just those detailees who make at least $100,000. Click the drop-down arrow next to Salary, then pick Number Filters | Greater Than Or Equal To and a dialog box appears. Enter 100000 (no dollar sign or commas) in the box on the right and click OK.

Excel shows us the 22 detailees who earned $100,000 or more.

	A Name	B Status	C Salary
19	Baker, Lamar W.	Detailee	$134999.
30	Berrigan, Elizabeth D.	Detailee	$152635.
51	Calderon, Tovah R.	Detailee	$155500.
64	Clark, Melanca D.	Detailee	$140259.
86	Dawe, Christopher J.	Detailee	$136134.
111	Fazili, Sameera	Detailee	$132009.
114	Ferrell, Taylor N.	Detailee	$136134.
149	Gunja, Mushtaq Z.	Detailee	$100206.
224	Lee, Marisa R.	Detailee	$105211.
230	Leonard, Shelley D.	Detailee	$123758.
251	Marquez, Laura R.	Detailee	$132009.
270	McQuaid, Nicholas L.	Detailee	$117637.
273	Mehrbani, Rodin A.	Detailee	$132009.
283	Montoya, Elisa D.	Detailee	$162400.
286	Morales, Esther F.	Detailee	$108717.
287	Morales, Ricardo O.	Detailee	$116535.
314	Parker, JaLynda L.	Detailee	$108717.
347	Riesen, Peter A.	Detailee	$148510.
368	Samuelson, Heather F.	Detailee	$123758.
384	Sharma, Avin P.	Detailee	$119238.
416	Thurston, Robin F.	Detailee	$119238.
443	Wheeler, Seth F.	Detailee	$225000.

2013 Report to Congress on Whi

READY   22 OF 460 RECORDS FOUND

Note: Filtered results.

We can filter on even more columns. We could even build filters that search a range of salaries or even a few characters inside a text field.

Any filter is a temporary view of data in Excel. If we want to create a permanent copy we must copy our filtered results and then paste them into a new sheet.

Copy these filtered rows by left clicking on the 1 for Row 1 and then dragging down to Row 443. Right-click anywhere on your selected data and pick Copy. If you're successful, you'll see pulsing dotted bars around your cells.

	A	B	C	D
1	**Name**	**Status**	**Salary**	**Pay Basis**
19	Baker, Lamar W.	Detailee	$134999.00	Per Annum
30	Berrigan, Elizabeth D.	Detailee	$152635.00	Per Annum
51	Calderon, Tovah R.	Detailee	$155500.00	Per Annum
64	Clark, Melanca D.	Detailee	$140259.00	Per Annum
86	Dawe, Christopher J.	Detailee	$136134.00	Per Annum
111	Fazili, Sameera	Detailee	$132009.00	Per Annum
114	Ferrell, Taylor N.	Detailee	$136134.00	Per Annum
149	Gunja, Mushtaq Z.	Detailee	$100206.00	Per Annum
224	Lee, Marisa R.	Detailee	$105211.00	Per Annum
230	Leonard, Shelley D.	Detailee	$23758.00	Per Annum
251	Marquez, Laura R.	Detailee	$132009.00	Per Annum
270	McQuaid, Nicholas L.	Detailee	$17637.00	Per Annum
273	Mehrbani, Rodin A.	Detailee	$132009.00	Per Annum
283	Montoya, Elisa D.	Detailee	$162400.00	Per Annum

Source: The White House.

Note: Filtered records selected.

Create a new sheet by clicking on the plus button near the active worksheet tab at the bottom. Now put your cursor in Cell A1 of the new sheet and Paste. Success! The new data with the detailees now appear in our new sheet. Widen the columns so you can see all the data.

Save the sheet and close it.

	A	B	C	D	E	F	G
1	**Name**	**Status**	**Salary**	**Pay Basis**	**Position Title**		
2	Baker, Lar	Detailee	#######	Per Annum	ASSOCIATE COUNSEL		
3	Berrigan, E	Detailee	#######	Per Annum	ETHICS COUNSEL		
4	Calderon,	Detailee	#######	Per Annum	SENIOR POLICY ADVISOR		
5	Clark, Mel	Detailee	#######	Per Annum	SENIOR POLICY ADVISOR		
6	Dawe, Chr	Detailee	#######	Per Annum	POLICY ADVISOR FOR HEALTH		
7	Fazili, San	Detailee	#######	Per Annum	SENIOR POLICY ADVISOR		
8	Ferrell, Tay	Detailee	#######	Per Annum	DEPUTY ASSOCIATE COUNSE		
9	Gunja, Mu	Detailee	#######	Per Annum	DEPUTY ASSOCIATE COUNSE		
10	Lee, Maris	Detailee	#######	Per Annum	SENIOR POLICY ADVISOR		
11	Leonard, S	Detailee	#######	Per Annum	CLEARANCE COUNSEL		
12	Marquez, I	Detailee	#######	Per Annum	OUTREACH AND RECRUITMEN		
13	McQuaid,	Detailee	#######	Per Annum	DEPUTY ASSOCIATE COUNSE		
14	Mehrbani,	Detailee	#######	Per Annum	DOMESTIC DIRECTOR FOR PR		
15	Montoya,	Detailee	#######	Per Annum	NATIONAL SECURITY DIRECTO		
16	Morales, E	Detailee	#######	Per Annum	ASSOCIATE DIRECTOR FOR PC		

Source: The White House.

Note: Filtered results pasted into a new spreadsheet.

GROUPING AND SUMMARIZING

In Chapter 6, we used Excel's pivot table function to run simple integrity checks that gave us a better understanding of the values in each of our data columns. Here, we will use pivot tables to answer "How much?" or "How many" questions about categories that we find in our data. For instance, we could have used pivot tables to determine whether detailees or employees on the White House staff get paid more on average.

We will now use pivot tables to answer questions about methamphetamine samples that were seized by law enforcement agencies worldwide in 2007 and later tested by the U.S. Drug Enforcement Administration. Download the stride_meth.xlsx Excel file on the book website. The author obtained the spreadsheet from the DEA website at http://www.justice.gov/dea/resource-center/stride-data.shtml and modified it for this exercise. The DEA extracts the data from its System to Retrieve Information from Drug Evidence II, an information system used to monitor trends in drug law enforcement operations (Drug Enforcement Administration, n.d.a). The DEA delays release of the data, because it says that it does not want to jeopardize active investigations (Drug Enforcement Administration, n.d.b).

Open the spreadsheet and note that it has 6,300 rows, including one for headers. Our columns include the state or country where the methamphetamines were seized, how the law enforcement agency obtained the drugs, the name of the drug, the potency on a scale of 1 to 100, the weight, and the year and month in which the drugs were seized. We'll use pivot tables to determine which state or country had the greatest number of seizures submitted to the DEA, which had the most meth by weight and which had the most potent meth on average.

Insert a pivot table into a new worksheet. Drop State/Country into the Row fields area and the state and country abbreviations appear in alphabetical order. Then drop State/County in the Value fields area and Excel counts the number of times each state or country appears in our data. AK for Alaska is at the top with 19.

To put the state or country with the highest number at the top, click in any of the cells with a number, then right-click and pick Sort I Sort Largest to Smallest in the popup menu. California (CA) is tops with 1,385, followed by Texas (TX) with 580. These states are number 1 and 2 in total population, so it shouldn't surprise us to see them at the top of our list. If we wanted to put these numbers into context, we would generate rates for all of the states using their populations.

Use File I Save As to save a working copy of the spreadsheet. Return to Sheet 1 to create a second pivot table. Drop State/Country into the row field area and then Potency into the value field area. Excel automatically sums the potency, which is not helpful because states with more test results could have higher sums. We want to generate an average, instead, to see which states or countries had highest potency in their seized meth. Click on the drop-down arrow to the right of Sum of Potency and select Average from the list that appears.

Sort the numbers descending to see which state or country had the highest potency. Australia (AS) is at the top with 85 percent, followed by Saipan, Mariana Islands (TT) at a little more than 80 percent. Massachusetts (MA) is third with nearly 76 percent.

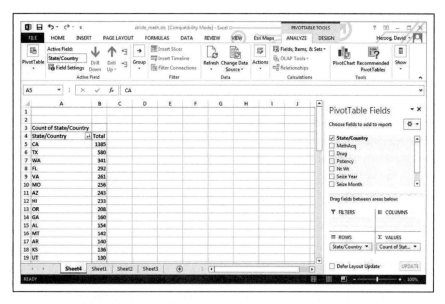

Source: Drug Enforcement Administration.

Note: Pivot table puts data into groups and summarizes.

We might want to have some context here so we can see if some of the higher averages might have resulted from one high test. So add the count of the State/Territory as a second data value field. Save your spreadsheet.

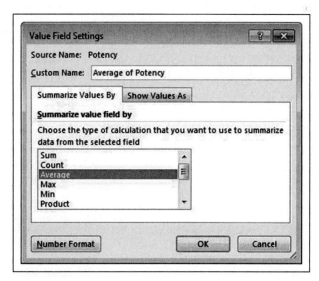

Source: Microsoft Excel for Windows 2013.

Note: Value fields settings dialog box.

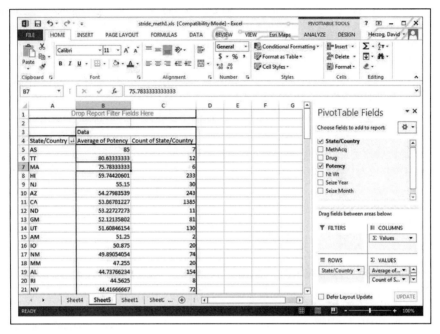

Source: Drug Enforcement Administration.

Note: Pivot table showing average meth average potency by state or country. Count added to provide context.

Last, we are going to figure out which state had the most seized meth sent to the DEA for testing. Go back to Sheet 1 and create another pivot table. Put State/Country into the

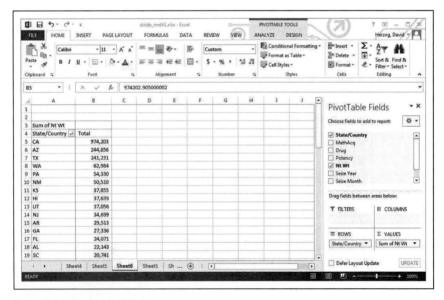

Source: Drug Enforcement Administration.

Note: Meth totals by state or country.

row fields area and Nt Wt into the value fields. Excel sums the weights for each State/Country. Sort and format the data as numbers using commas. Meth from California (CA) was the most tested by total weight at 974,203 pounds.

Save your file and close it.

In this chapter, we learned how to manipulate data by sorting, filtering and using pivot tables to create summaries for groups. Experienced data users typically use database manager programs, such as Microsoft Access and MySQL, to create these groups and summaries. However, we can perform many of the same functions using spreadsheets.

This wraps up the data analysis section of the book. In this section, we learned why it's important to place numbers into context, and how to put them in context by comparing them to others. We also learned how to calculate those comparisons as amount change, percent change, percent of total, rates, ratios and averages.

In the next section, we dive into how visualization can help reveal patterns in our data and communicate our results to others.

ON YOUR OWN

Using the stride_meth.xlsx file, answer these questions for California only: (1) In which month did the DEA receive the greatest number of meth seizures? (2) In which month did the DEA get the most meth, by weight? (3) In which month was the meth that California sent to the DEA the most potent? Filter your data and use pivot tables to answer these questions.

CHAPTER 11   VISUALIZING YOUR DATA

D ata visualization has been all the rage recently, as Web-based tools have made it easier to display data and share them with others. But data visualization has been used for decades as a means to help understand data patterns and communicate those to others. The goal of this section of the book is to provide a solid footing in the fundamentals of data visualization. This section will touch on some best practices that have been refined over the years and some options for visualizing data accurately. Additionally, in this section we'll learn how to create a number of different types of visualizations using Excel's charting functions and online services offered by Google. We start this section with Chapter 11, where we will explore some principles that will help us better understand data visualization.

DATA VISUALIZATION DEFINED

Visualization is simply the act of creating charts based on data. We can easily visualize a small data set, such as a spreadsheet file. Data scientists, using other tools, can visualize terabytes of more-complex data (sometimes called "big data") from social networks, such as Twitter and Facebook, to better understand the flow of information about disasters or news events.

At their simplest, data visualizations can be barebones representations of data. Many times, analysts visualize data just for themselves, so they can get a better understanding of their data. Sometimes it's difficult to detect interesting or meaningful patterns by looking at columns and rows of data. In fact, data analysts will often create many different visualizations that can help show the data from different perspectives, or they will show a subset of the data. The techniques of **exploratory data analysis**, as promoted by statistician John Tukey, use different types of graphs to get a better understanding (Tukey, 1977). Some statistical programs, such as SPSS, JMP, MATLAB and the open source R, have exploratory data analysis functions. Excel's charting tools allow us to accomplish many of the same basic goals, albeit with more effort.

If we want to communicate to a specific audience, we might choose to create an **information graphic**—a more elegant representation. We could use a graphic design program like Adobe Illustrator to create a static information graphic, or we could use an interactive visualization tool like Tableau Desktop. The art of crafting information graphics is outside the scope of this book. To learn more, read *The Functional Art* by Alberto Cairo (2013), *Visualize This* by Nathan Yau (2011), or the books of Edward Tufte (1983, 2006).

Regardless of whether we're creating a visualization for ourselves or for others, our goal is to emphasize the content, and to help it tell a story.

"Graphics, charts, and maps are not just tools to be seen, but to be read and scrutinized. The first goal of an infographic is not to be beautiful just for the sake of eye appeal, but, above all, to be understandable first, and beautiful after that; or to be beautiful because of its exquisite functionality," wrote Cairo (2013, xx).

In the words of information design guru Tufte, "Graphics reveal data" (1983, 13). Many information designers have gravitated toward Tufte's ideas, which emphasize simplicity. In 1983, he issued his theory of graphical excellence, which includes instructions to

Show the data

Induce the viewer to think about the substance rather than about the methodology, graphic design, the technology of the graphic production, or something else

Avoid distorting what the data have to say

Present many numbers in a small space

Make large data sets coherent

Encourage the eye to compare different pieces of data

Reveal the data at several levels of detail, from broad overview to the fine structure

Serve a reasonably clear purpose: description, exploration, tabulation or decoration

Be closely integrated with the statistical and verbal descriptions of a data set (Tufte, 1983).

Reprinted with permission by Edward R. Tufte, Graphics Press Cheshire, CT.

SOME BEST PRACTICES

Here, then, are some quick guidelines for creating visualizations, whether they're for yourself, another person or a broader audience.

Give your chart a title. Use just a few words to describe what's displayed. Include the time frame for your data (e.g., "State unemployment rate, 2000–2012").

Label your chart elements. That includes the vertical and horizontal axes, legends and any other elements.

Include a source line. A source line reminds you about where you obtained the data. If you're sharing your visualization, it shows others where you got the data. This is important because you want to give others the ability to try to replicate or even challenge your results.

Display enough data to provide context. For instance, showing only three years of unemployment data might mask the fact that the rate had been rising in earlier years.

Let's look at this example of an Excel column chart that was created relatively quickly by the author. Using data downloaded from the St. Louis Federal Reserve Bank's FRED service, it shows how the U.S. GDP has changed from 2000 through early 2013. The GDP

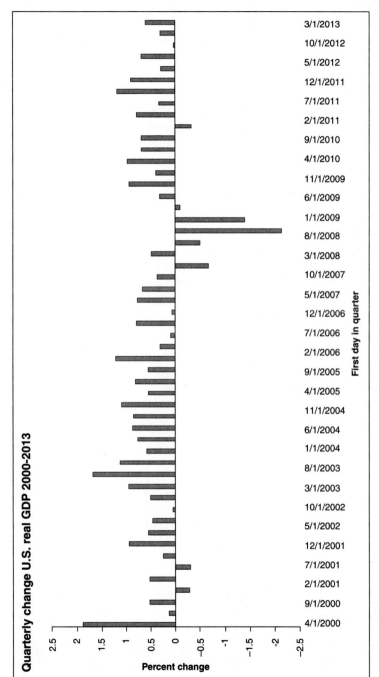

Quarterly change U.S. real GDP 2000-2013

First day in quarter

Percent change

Source: Department of Commerce, Retrieved from http://research.stlouisfed.org/fred2/graph/?id=GDPC1.

Note: Excel column chart.

is an important measure that's used to determine whether the U.S. economy is growing and includes "the output of goods and services produced by labor and property located in the United States" (Bureau of Economic Analysis, 2014). The U.S. Department of Commerce's Bureau of Economic Analysis releases the data quarterly. We can easily see by looking at this chart how the GDP in the United States began shrinking in 2007, as the global financial crisis began.

Note that the chart title says, "Quarterly change U.S. Real GDP 2000–2013." This communicates to viewers that the data are reported quarterly and expressed in terms of real dollars. We prefer to use data based on real dollars because doing so takes into account the effects of inflation. The title also signals to viewers they are looking at data spanning the years 2000 to 2013.

Our source line, placed just below the title, tells the viewers that the BEA produced these data and gives them the link on FRED, in the event that they'd like to retrieve the data themselves.

The vertical axis label shows viewers that the change is reported as percent, with the axis scale ranging from 2.5 percent growth to 2.5 percent loss.

The horizontal axis label tells viewers that each column represents the first day in a quarter. The labels themselves mention the specific dates. Note that the St. Louis Fed adjusts all quarterly dates to the first date of the quarter (Federal Reserve Bank of St. Louis, n.d.). Our data contain more than a decade of information, which is enough to show the big picture of GDP growth and loss during those years.

Now that we've seen some of the best practices in action, it's time to learn which chart options are the best for displaying different kinds of data.

CHAPTER 12 **CHARTING CHOICES**

W hen creating data visualizations, part of the challenge is picking the right type of chart. Excel gives us around a dozen options, everything from the simple pie chart to sparklines. So, the big question becomes, Which option should we choose? That is, which will be the most appropriate and communicate the best? The answer depends on the kind of data that we want to visualize. Here is a guide to the chart options and the data types that they're best suited to display.

VISUALIZING DATA WITH CHARTS

Pie charts are the best tool for showing proportions of the whole. These charts are the visual equivalent of using a spreadsheet to calculate the percent of total. As long as you use a limited number of categories, pie charts can make it easy for people to understand proportions. For instance, this pie chart from a report by the U.S. Consumer Financial Protection Bureau shows us that nearly half of complaints received by the Bureau were about mortgages, at 48 percent. Complaints about credit cards, the next largest category, came in at 21 percent of the total. Student loans made up just a sliver at 3 percent (Consumer Financial Protection Bureau, n.d.a).

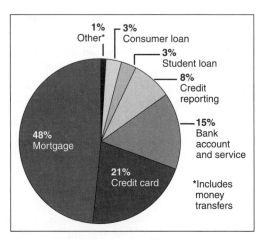

Source: A snapshot of complaints received. (n.d.). Consumer Financial Protection Bureau. Retrieved July 11, 2013, from http://www.consumerfinance.gov/reports/a-snapshot-of-complaints-received-3/

Note: Pie chart showing proportion of consumer complaints reported to federal authorities.

Likewise, this pie chart from a federal spending report tells us an awful lot about how the U.S. government spent its money in fiscal year 2012. Roughly two-thirds (66 percent) of all spending was by the Social Security Administration, Department of Health and Human Services and the Department of Defense (Financial Management Service, 2013).

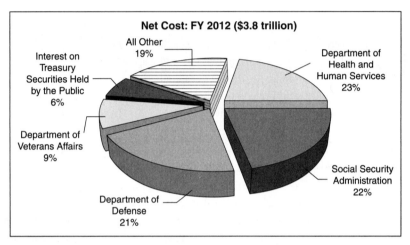

Source: Current report: Combined Statement of Receipts, Outlays and Balances. Financial Management Service. (n.d.) **Web.** Retrieved from http://www.fiscal.treasury.gov/fsreports/rpt/combStmt/cs2012/outlay.pdf

Note: 3-D pie charts distort data. The slice for the Department of Defense in the front looks bigger than the one for the Department of Health and Human Services in the back, but the Department of Defense's share is actually 2 percentage points less.

Pie charts have come under attack lately because they sometimes fail to make the data more understandable (Hickey, 2013). As Hickey suggests, avoid the temptation to create 3-D pie charts (such as the one above) because they can distort results and make some pie slices appear bigger than they ought to be.

Vertical **column charts** are ideal for showing change over time when you have discrete **time-series data**. Discrete time-series data are reported at defined intervals. Some examples include the quarterly GDP data we saw visualized in Chapter 11, monthly unemployment figures and annual four-year college tuition costs.

We can even create stacked vertical column charts to show proportions over time. For instance, this chart visualizes not only the increase in enrollment at full-time degree-granting institutions, but also the growing share of women attending college.

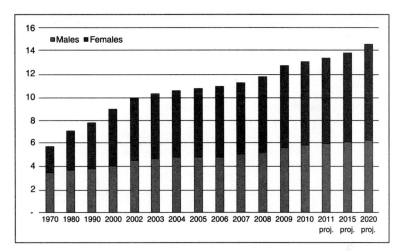

Source: National Center for Education Statistics, Department of Education, Retrieved from http://nces.ed.gov/programs/digest/d11/tables/dt1.

Note: Stacked vertical column chart showing proportions over time.

Clustered column charts allow us to compare categories over time by placing columns side by side. This clustered column chart provides a different view of our enrollment data. This one shows even better how the gap between female and male students has been widening.

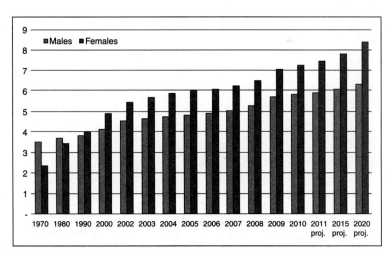

Source: National Center for Education Statistics, Department of Education, Retrieved from http://nces.ed.gov/programs/digest/d11/tables/dt1.

Note: Clustered vertical column chart compares categories over time.

Line charts are a great choice when we have continuous time-series data. Continuous data are those that represent processes or conditions that occur continuously, such as the outdoor temperatures. The use of the line is more appropriate because it suggests an ongoing phenomenon. In this chart, a line represents the hourly temperatures recorded by the National Weather Service in Pittsburgh, Pennsylvania, on September 1, 2013, found at http://www.erh.noaa.gov/pbz/hourlyclimate.htm.

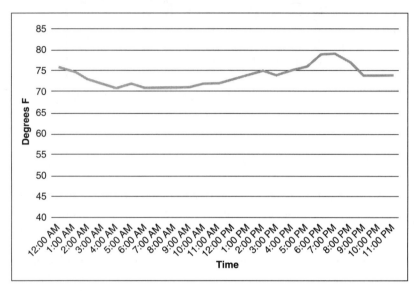

Source: National Weather Service, Retrieved from http://www.erh.noaa.gov/pbz/hourlyclimate.htm.

Note: Line charts show continuous time-series data, such as temperature readings.

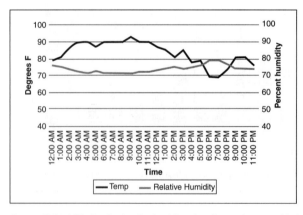

Source: National Weather Service. Retrieved from http://www.erh.noaa.gov/pbz/hourlyclimate.htm.

Note: More than one data element displayed on a line chart.

If we have more than one data element that we'd like to chart to add context or make comparisons, we can add more lines. With this chart, data about relative humidity by the hour in Pittsburgh have been added. Note that these data are plotted on the same scale as the temperature.

We can choose horizontal **bar charts** when

we want data that are categorized in just a few ways. For instance, this bar chart shows us the number of higher-education degrees granted in the United States 2009–2010. This chart works well because we have a small number of categories. It could get difficult to understand if we had too many.

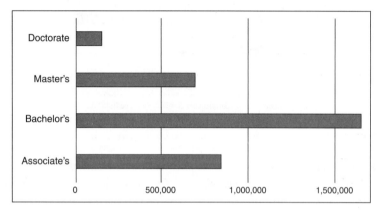

Source: National Center for Education Statistics, Department of Education. Retrieved from http://nces.ed.gov/programs/digest/d11/tables/dt11_283.asp?referrer=report.

Note: Data categories shown on a horizontal bar chart.

As we did with the vertical columns chart earlier, we can show proportions by using stacked bars. The first chart below shows not only the total number of degrees, but also the proportion of women and men who earned them. We could also use a clustered bar chart to compare the degrees earned by men and women in yet another way.

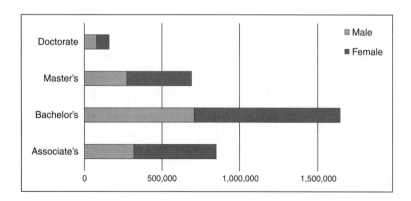

Source: National Center for Education Statistics, Department of Education. Retrieved from http://nces.ed.gov/programs/digest/d11/tables/dt11_283.asp?referrer=report.

Note: Showing proportion with a stacked bar chart.

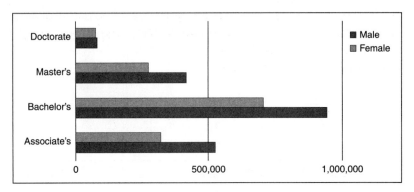

Source: National Center for Education Statistics, Department of Education. Retrieved from http://nces.ed.gov/programs/digest/d11/tables/dt11_283.asp?referrer=report.

Note: Comparing categories with a clustered bar chart.

Scatterplots help us show whether we might have a relationship between two data variables. For instance, we could plot SAT or ACT scores against college freshman grade point averages to see whether there is any relationship between high scores on those standardized tests and student performance. The scatterplot below uses the crime data from Chapter 9 and shows the relationship between property crimes (the horizontal axis) and violent crimes (the vertical axis). In general, we see that as the number of property crimes increases, so does the number of violent crimes. The chart includes a linear **trend line** that shows the central tendency of the data. Any point that's well above the trend line represents a city whose violent crime numbers are higher than expected. Excel uses a statistical calculation called **linear regression** to determine the position of the linear trend line.

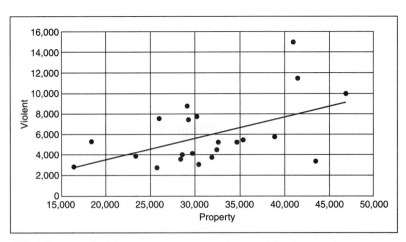

Source: Federal Bureau of Investigation. Retrieved from http://www.fbi.gov/about-us/cjis/ucr/ucr-publications#Crime.

Note: Scatterplots for comparing variables.

Stock charts—or boxplots—can be used to visualize the performance of stocks over time. Many times, we see stock price data visualized as a line chart, but the stock chart can provide more detail than a simple line chart. Here we see monthly Google stock opening and closing prices, as represented by the inner bars. The outer lines display the high and low prices.

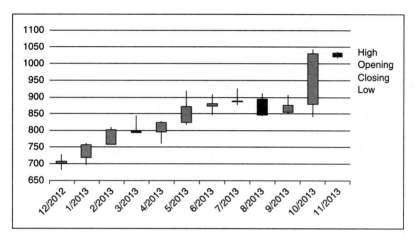

Source: Yahoo Finance. Retrieved from http://finance.yahoo.com/q/hp?s=GOOG&a=07&b=19&c=2004&d=10&e=6&f=2013&g=m&z=66&y=66.

Note: Stock chart, otherwise known as a boxplot.

Sparklines are "intense, simple, word-sized graphics" (Tufte, 2006, 47) that are a relatively new charting option in Excel spreadsheets. Sparklines are placed inside individual cells and take the place of numbers or text. In Excel, we can create line, bar and win-loss sparklines. The sparklines in the spreadsheet here show how median income has changed from 1995 to 2011 for men and women, and by level of education. A sparkline is an excellent tool for helping compare patterns in large data sets.

Source: National Center for Education Statistics, Department of Education.

Note: Sparklines are repetitive charts that fit inside cells.

Finally, a map is often the best way to visualize **geographic data**. Viewers can orient themselves and understand what's happening near them. Out of the box, Excel is unable to create maps but can do so using plug-in programs. We can use **geographic information system** (GIS) programs, such as ArcGIS or Quantum GIS, to create data maps. Or we can use online programs, such as Google Fusion Tables. This Fusion Table map shows the location of residences where the Columbia (Missouri) Police Department responded to reports of nuisance parties. Most of the points are concentrated in areas with large amounts of student housing.

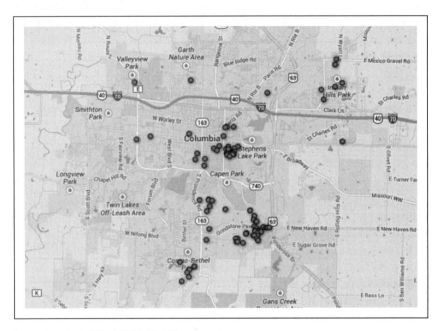

Source: Google maps; City of Columbia, Missouri.

Note: A Google Fusion Table map.

Now that we know which charts are the best for our data, we're going to learn in the next chapter how to build these charts in Excel.

ON YOUR OWN

Find three charts or information graphics in print or on the Internet. Write a critique of each: How easy is it for you to understand? Was the chart the best choice for the data? Why or why not? Did the chart have the necessary elements? Make sure you provide a copy of each chart or a URL for it.

N ow we will use Excel to create the charts that we saw in Chapter 12. Download the charting.xlsx file from the website for this book and open it. It contains seven worksheets, which have labels on their tabs. The first one is Degrees conferred. This sheet, like all of the others, has data that have been edited and formatted so it's easier to create the charts. Often, the data we want to use for our charts are stored in columns or rows that aren't neighbors. That makes it challenging to highlight just what we need. The data sources are noted at the bottom of each sheet and include URLs for download.

PIE CHART

We'll start by creating a pie chart to show the proportion of degrees conferred in 2009–2010, using data from the National Center for Education Statistics. The first two rows hold the data we

need to build the chart. It has the degree category in the first row and the numbers for each category in the second.

Highlight cells A1 through E2. Then select the Insert tab and click on the drop-down arrow for the pie chart button.

Select the 2-D Pie option and Excel creates the chart just like that.

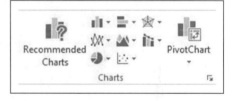

Source: Microsoft Excel for Windows 2013.

Note: Excel chart type selector.

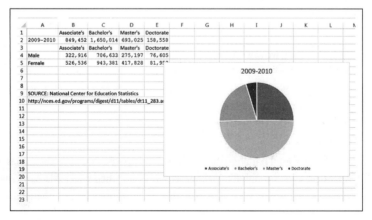

Source: National Center for Education Statistics, Department of Education.

Note: Creating a pie chart.

The chart is not very descriptive as it stands, so we are going to add some elements that will help viewers make sense of it. Double-click on the chart title at the top; now we can edit it. Let's change the text to, "College degrees conferred 2009–2010". The legend, which contains the color key for each degree, is at the bottom of the chart. Let's move that to the right of our pie. Click on the legend to resize and move it.

Finally, we'll add a source line below the pie so we can cite the NCES and provide a URL to the data. Click on the Format tab and then look for the Insert Shapes tool on the left. Select the Text Box tool and then use your cursor to enter the source information on the first line and the URL on the second. Resize the pie chart area if there is not enough room for the source line. Our finished chart should look like this:

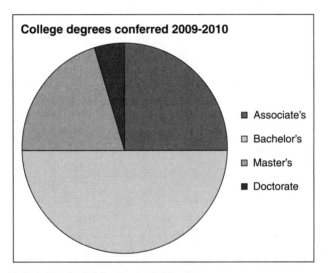

Source: National Center for Education Statistics, Department of Education.

Note: Pie chart with title, legend and source line.

Examining this chart, we can see that nearly half of all degrees awarded were bachelor's degrees. Associate's degrees make up about one quarter; master's and doctorate degrees, combined, make up another quarter. We've done some work, so let's create a working copy of this file by picking File | Save As.

HORIZONTAL BAR CHARTS

We can also use horizontal bar charts if we want to compare our degree categories. Once again, highlight cells A1 through E2. Pick Insert Bar Chart, then select 2-D Bar, Clustered Bar. Excel creates this chart. We could edit this if we wanted by modifying the chart

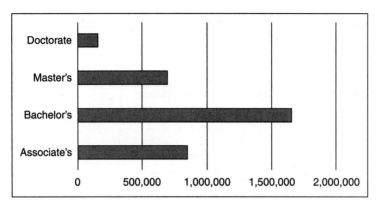

Source: National Center for Education Statistics, Department of Education.
Note: Horizontal bar chart.

title and adding a source line. Excel has automatically chosen to use degree numbers in increments of 500,000 for the horizontal axis labels.

Right below our table we have another that breaks down the degrees earned by sex. Highlight cells A4 to E6. Insert a Bar Chart and pick Stacked. That will create the same chart with four bars, this time showing the shares earned by women and by men.

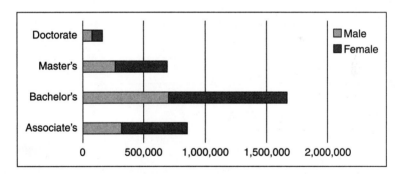

Source: National Center for Education Statistics, Department of Education.
Note: Stacked horizontal bar chart shows proportions.

As we saw in Chapter 12, the clustered bar chart allowed us to see the differences more clearly. So let's build that. Instead of creating a new chart from scratch, we can right-click on the chart area and then pick Change Chart Type. . . . Pick Clustered Bar from the box that appears and Excel creates this chart. It's much easier to see the differences between the sexes with this one.

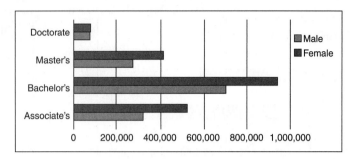

Source: National Center for Education Statistics, Department of Education.

Note: Clustered horizontal bar chart compares categories.

COLUMN AND LINE CHARTS

Now that we've charted categorical data from one point in time, we are going to learn how to chart time-series data. Remember that we have two choices when charting time-series data: (1) column charts for data that were recorded or reported at discrete points in time, and (2) line charts for data that measure a continuous phenomenon, such as the weather.

We'll use the GDP data on the GDP sheet to create our first column chart. The GDP data are reported quarterly, as reflected by the dates stored in column A. Column B tells us the percentage change from the previous quarter.

Highlight A1 through B54 to grab the data that we need to create our chart. Insert a 2-D Clustered Column chart. Excel creates a barebones chart that lacks a lot of descriptive information. Also, we see that our horizontal axis labels have been stuffed into the middle of the chart, making them difficult to read.

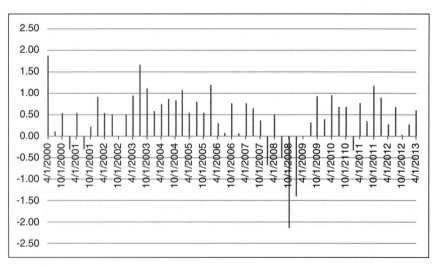

Source: Department of Commerce, retrieved from FRED.

Note: Vertical column chart.

We're going to clean this chart up and discover some tricks that we can use later. First, let's fix the position of the horizontal axis labels. Select the labels and then go to the Format Axis Box that appears. Pick the column chart button and open the Labels item. Use the drop-down to pick Low as the label position.

Now we will label both of our axes, so chart viewers can understand what each means. Pick Add Chart Element from the Design tab and then Axis Titles | Primary Vertical. A text box appears. Enter "Percent change". Likewise, create a horizontal axis label that says "Quarter". Retitle the chart to "Quarterly change, U.S. real GDP 2000–2013".

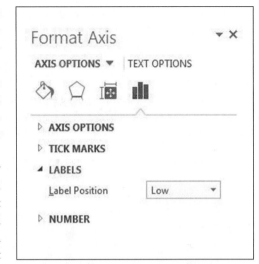

Source: Microsoft Excel for Windows 2013.

Note: Format axis settings.

Last, we want to insert a source line. Right now we don't have enough room at the bottom of the chart. We can resize the chart plot area to free up some space. Click on the plot area and resizing handles appear. Drag them to make the plot area smaller.

Now it looks much better, and someone can understand what it means.

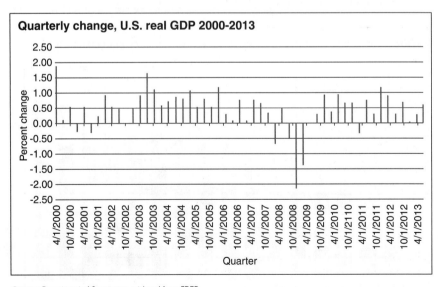

Source: Department of Commerce, retrieved from FRED.

Note: Category labels placed at bottom of axis.

Our next column charts will be those in which we'll display fall enrollment at U.S. degree-granting institutions of higher education over time. Go to the Enrollment tab to find these data from the NCES. Row 1 holds the categories for years. Rows 2 and 3 hold enrollment data that the author has reformatted so the vertical axis labels appear properly when charting. The numbers are in millions, rounded up to whole numbers. The original numbers appear in Rows 4 and 5 and are reported in thousands.

Highlight cells A1 through S3 and insert a Stacked Column chart to create this chart. Our chart shows increased enrollment since the 1970s, with women increasing their share.

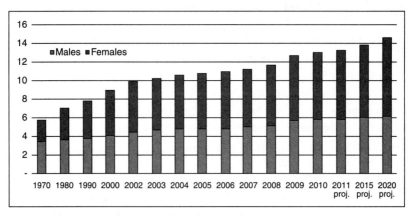

Source: National Center for Education Statistics, Department of Education.

Note: Stacked vertical column chart.

Use Change Chart Type and pick Clustered Column. We see that more men than women had enrolled in 1970. Sometime in the 1980s women surpassed men. We can see that the current gap is expected to widen even more during the coming years.

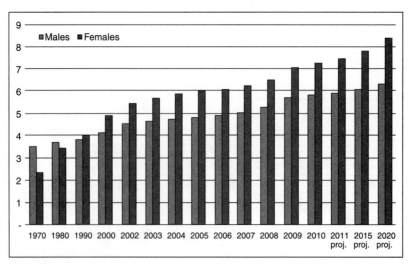

Source: National Center for Education Statistics, Department of Education.

Note: Clustered vertical column chart.

Let's turn to charting using continuous time series data. Go to the PBGH Weather sheet, which has hourly temperature and relative humidity data from September 1, 2013; the author downloaded these data from the National Weather Service. First, we will plot just one variable, the temperature. Then we will add the humidity readings.

Select cells A1 through B25 and insert a 2-D Line Chart. This chart appears. It looks like the temperatures bounced around a lot on that date. That's because the bottom value on the vertical axis is 66 degrees. We can set that to a lower value to render a more accurate picture of the temperature on that date.

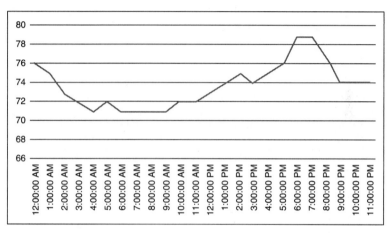

Source: National Weather Service.

Note: Line chart. Note that the temperatures appear more extreme than they were because the vertical axis starts at 66 degrees.

Select the vertical axis labels and then, in the Format Axis box, set the Bounds Minimum to 40. The chart now looks much better.

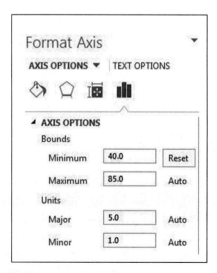

Source: Microsoft Excel for Windows 2013.

Note: Modify axis in vertical axis setting.

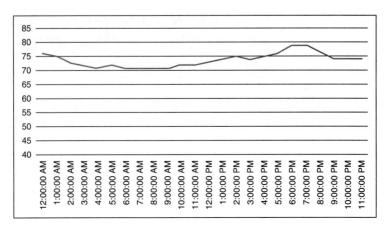

Source: National Weather Service.

Note: Temperature variation smoothed, thanks to vertical axis minimum lowered to 40 degrees.

Next we will create a chart that has the temperature and relative humidity. Select Cells A1 through C25 and insert a 2-D Line Chart. We get this chart, which shows both, plotted on the same 0- to 100-point scale. Of course, we could modify that scale if we wanted to.

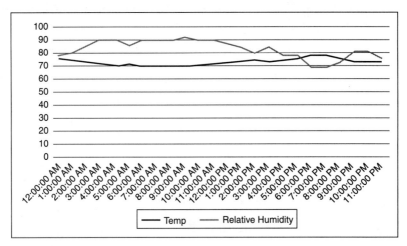

Source: National Weather Service.

Note: Line for relative humidity added to chart.

SCATTERPLOT

For our next chart we will again plot two variables. As we learned in the previous chapter, scatterplots can help us see whether there is a relationship between numeric variables. Go to the Crimes worksheet, which has data about property crimes and violent crimes in cities with populations 500,000 to 999,999. Highlight the cells containing the data—B1 through C23— and then pick Insert Scatter, using the first option. From the distribution of the points, it does look like there is a relationship between the number of property and violent crimes.

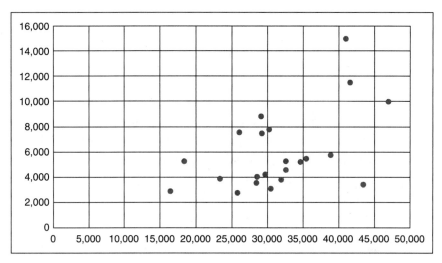

Source: Federal Bureau of Investigation.

Note: Scatterplot of property and violent crimes.

Change the title to "Crimes 2012". Label the horizontal axis "Property" and the vertical axis "Violent". No city has fewer than 16,000 property crimes, so change the minimum bounds for that axis to 15000. Our chart looks better now.

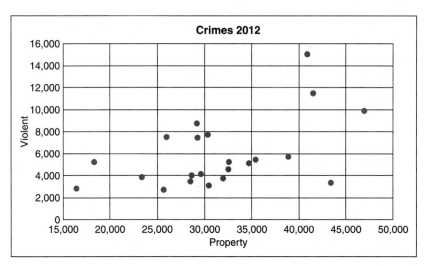

Source: Federal Bureau of Investigation.

Note: Scatterplot with new horizontal axis settings and labels.

Let's add a finishing touch, a linear trend line. Excel uses a statistical function called linear regression to draw the line that's a best fit for the data. Points that are very high above the line represent cities with more violent crimes than we would expect, based on their numbers of property crimes.

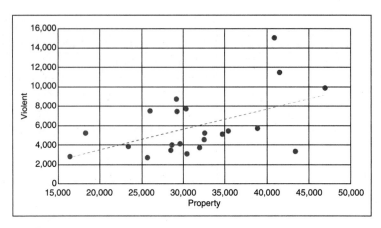

Source: Federal Bureau of Investigation.

Note: Scatterplot with linear trend line showing the central tendency.

STOCK CHART

Pick the Google stock sheet, which contains monthly performance data downloaded from Yahoo Finance. Note that when we create stock charts our data need to be ordered properly: date, opening price, high price, low price and closing price. Date represents the first day of trading for each month. Highlight cells A1 through E15 and Insert Stock, Surface or Radar Chart (the one that looks like a spiderweb). Then pick the Open-High-Low-Close option. Change the vertical axis label's minimum bounds to 600 to eliminate the empty space at the bottom. This also allows us to better distinguish how the stock performed in each month. We see that some of our inner bars, which display the closing and opening prices, are filled in. That's Excel's way of telling us that the stock closing price fell below its opening price in those months.

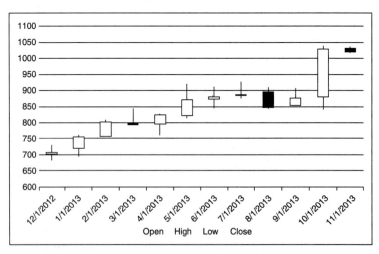

Source: Yahoo Finance.

Note: Stock chart showing opening, closing, high and low prices.

SPARKLINES

We'll wrap up this chapter by learning how to create sparklines. Pick the Median income tab to find data from the NCES. We have nine columns of salary amounts in different years and more than 50 categories. The procedure for creating sparklines is a little more involved than for the other charts we've created so far. Click on the Line button in the Sparklines group and then set the Data Range to B2:J67. Next tell Excel where to put the sparklines. The Location Range needs to be K2:K67. Click OK and we've placed our sparklines in the K column.

2	All persons, all education levels	$36,900	$39,190	$37,990	$38,140	$37,970	$37,600	$39,800	$38,560	$37,950
3	Less than high school completion	23,400	23,640	23,660	22,320	23,780	22,330	21,850	21,660	22,860
4	High school completion\3\	30,680	32,650	32,130	32,290	31,420	31,310	31,370	30,850	29,950
5	Some college, no degree	34,310	37,680	36,140	35,020	35,660	33,390	34,780	33,940	31,990
6	Associate's degree	36,630	39,180	39,120	37,720	37,750	37,540	37,640	38,150	37,030
7	Bachelor's or higher degree	48,670	52,240	50,530	50,050	51,910	52,180	52,250	50,270	50,000
8	Bachelor's degree	45,700	52,130	46,990	48,520	48,630	48,060	47,170	46,420	44,970
9	Master's or higher degree	58,520	62,590	57,520	55,790	60,390	57,400	62,090	56,380	59,230

Source: National Center for Education Statistics, Department of Education.

Note: Sparklines.

That's it for our lesson on making Excel charts. In the next chapter, we'll wrap up this section on data visualization with a look at Web-based tools that allow us to create and share charts.

ON YOUR OWN

Download the Excel spreadsheet charting2.xlsx from the book website and use the data provided on each tab to create the best chart possible. Make a note of why you chose the particular chart type.

CHAPTER 14

CHARTING WITH WEB TOOLS

A s we saw in the last chapter, Excel is a powerful tool that we can use to create data visualizations for ourselves. Thanks to an explosion of Web 2.0 tools in the past several years, we have an abundance of options available for creating visualizations that we can share with the world. Numerous Web-based charting platforms have emerged, providing plenty of choices. Some of them have gained traction and developed a loyal user base, while others have been shuttered by their developers. In this chapter, we will take a look at some of the tools that have been around the longest and thus are more likely to be around in the coming years. These tools are powerful and allow us to create many of the same charts that we can make in Excel. Anyone with more-advanced Web design and development skills can create even richer data visualizations.

Before we learn about the tools, we're going to look at a few examples of interactive data visualizations that have been created with government data.

This visualization shows us how much money has been budgeted and spent by the Cook County, Illinois, government over 20 years. Cook County includes Chicago and a number

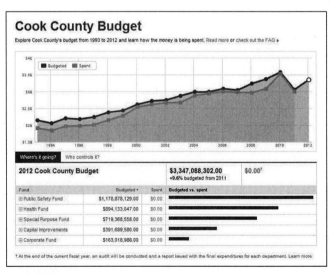

Source: Where's the money going? (n.d.). Look at Cook: Brought to you by Cook County Commissioner John Fritchey. Retrieved December 20, 2013, from http://lookatcook.com/

Note: Interactive visualization using government data.

of the city's suburbs. The line chart shows us that the city spends less money than it has budgeted in any given year. The bar chart at the bottom right shows us that the Public Safety Fund accounts for most of the spending, followed by the Health Fund. If we click on the plus signs to the left of any of the fund names, we can drill down and get more detailed data about that fund (Look at Cook, n.d.).

This visualization from the federal Consumer Financial Protection Bureau shows us mortgage application activity across the United States, using a map and column charts. The CFPB uses Home Mortgage Disclosure Act data for the visualization. We can set parameters to create customized charts that display mortgage activity for the Metropolitan Statistical Areas that interest us. Here, the author created a clustered column chart that shows mortgage activity in the MSA that includes Las Vegas, which was one of the country's hottest real estate markets a few years back (Consumer Financial Protection Bureau, n.d.b).

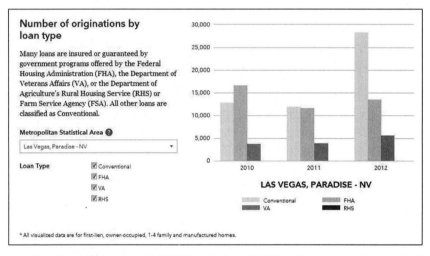

Source: Home Mortgage Disclosure Act. (n.d.). CFPB. Retrieved December 20, 2013, from http://www.consumerfinance.gov/hmda/
Note: Online data visualization using government mortgage application data.

Like many major U.S. cities, Houston has a 311 reporting system to help residents and businesses request services, such as sidewalk or pothole repairs. All of the requests for service, whether they're made by telephone or online, are entered into a master database. In addition to using the data to manage the requests, the city makes them available online and allows members of the public to create visualizations with the data. For example, a tree map created by the author shows that Nuisance on Property is the most common reason for complaints, at nearly 9 percent of all cases (City of Houston, n.d.).

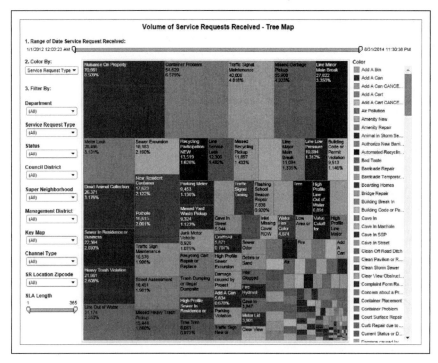

Source: City of Houston 311 Data Visualizations. (n.d.) Retrieved December 20, 2013, from http://performance.houstontx
.gov/311Dashboards

Note: Interactive tree map visualization of calls to Houston 311 center.

ONLINE VISUALIZATION OPTIONS

We have many options for creating visualizations that we can post on the Web and share. Some of them come from established technology companies, such as Google and IBM. Others come from relative newcomers like Infoactive and Infogram.

Google Spreadsheets offer one of the easiest to use and most robust charting options. Anyone with a Google Drive or Gmail account can create these spreadsheets and charts. In this example, the author has uploaded the charting.xlsx file that we used to create Excel charts in the previous chapter.

After highlighting the desired data range, we just click the Insert chart . . . button and Google Spreadsheets launches the Chart Editor, where we can customize our chart. After building the chart, we can pick Publish chart . . . from the drop-down arrow at the top right. From there we can get an **embed code** for an interactive chart that we can paste into a blog or other Web content management system.

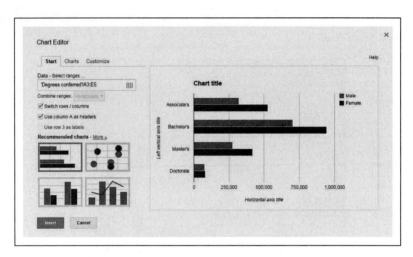

Source: National Center for Education Statistics, Department of Education.

Note: Stacked bar charts in Google Spreadsheets.

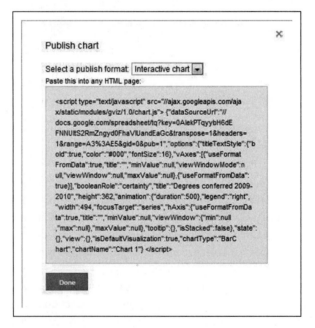

Source: Google Spreadsheets.

Note: Embed code used for publishing Google Spreadsheet chart.

Fusion Tables are the next step up in Google's data visualization tool kit. Fusion Tables technically are still in the experimental phase, but they've been a popular visualization tool for the past few years. Fusion Tables are more complex than Charts, but they also give us more flexibility in how we prepare and display our data.

For this example, the author used the existing Google Spreadsheet with the charting data and imported the table for the GDP change. After changing some settings, this chart resulted:

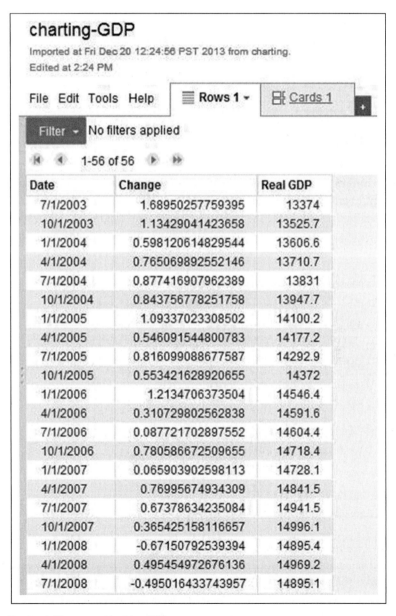

Date	Change	Real GDP
7/1/2003	1.68950257759395	13374
10/1/2003	1.13429041423658	13525.7
1/1/2004	0.598120614829544	13606.6
4/1/2004	0.765069892552146	13710.7
7/1/2004	0.877416907962389	13831
10/1/2004	0.843756778251758	13947.7
1/1/2005	1.09337023308502	14100.2
4/1/2005	0.546091544800783	14177.2
7/1/2005	0.816099088677587	14292.9
10/1/2005	0.553421628920655	14372
1/1/2006	1.2134706373504	14546.4
4/1/2006	0.310729802562838	14591.6
7/1/2006	0.087721702897552	14604.4
10/1/2006	0.780586672509655	14718.4
1/1/2007	0.065903902598113	14728.1
4/1/2007	0.76995674934309	14841.5
7/1/2007	0.67378634235084	14941.5
10/1/2007	0.365425158116657	14996.1
1/1/2008	-0.67150792539394	14895.4
4/1/2008	0.495454972676136	14969.2
7/1/2008	-0.495016433743957	14895.1

Source: Department of Commerce, retrieved from FRED.

Note: GDP data in a Google Fusion Table.

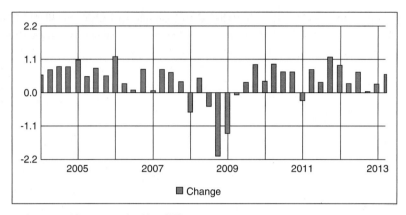

Source: Department of Commerce, retrieved from FRED.

Note: GDP data in a Google Fusion Table chart.

ManyEyes, from IBM, is another well-established data visualization platform that's widely used. After creating a free account, users can upload data by copying them from a spreadsheet and pasting them into a box. The author used the city crime data in the Charting spreadsheet to create this scatterplot to show the relationship between property and violent crimes.

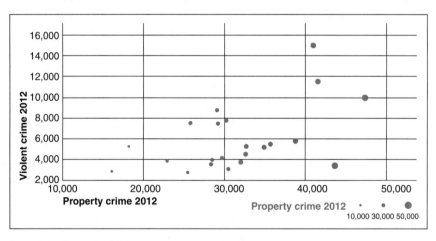

Source: Federal Bureau of Investigation.

Note: Crime scatterplot on ManyEyes.

EVALUATING WEB VISUALIZATION PLATFORMS

When evaluating Web-based data visualization platforms, it helps to consider potential strengths and weaknesses.

On the plus side, most of these Web tools are available at no cost. We don't have to purchase or license any software, unlike when we want to use a commercial program like Excel. In a similar vein, we don't need to download or install any software on our laptop. The company offering the visualization service runs the software for us in the cloud.

Another plus is that the service hosts our data. We don't need to worry about getting and keeping the data online. Moreover, the visualization platforms allow us to access our data wherever we are in the world. So, there are some very strong benefits to using these services.

However, there are some drawbacks to consider when using these tools. One big consideration is that you often surrender control of your data when you make it available on these sites. So make sure that you read the terms of service, which is a legally binding document that defines the relationship between you and the website. Also, read the privacy statement, which outlines how the website uses personal and other data that are submitted by users.

Some other drawbacks include downtime for Web applications. Even the most robust Web platforms fail on occasion. Whom can you call at Google if your Fusion Table charts suddenly go dark? A related risk is that the visualization platform could be taken offline completely. This, in fact, happened several years ago to Swivel.com, a popular visualization platform.

ManyEyes' and Google's offerings remain good choices because of their longevity and homes inside well-established tech companies.

CREATING FUSION TABLE CHARTS

To end this chapter, we are going to create some charts using Fusion Tables. You'll need to make sure that you have a Google account with Google Drive. Next, go to your Drive and upload the charting.xlsx Excel sheet. Convert it to the Google Docs format, if you are prompted. Now we are ready to create some Fusion Tables based on the data.

Launch Fusion Tables by visiting http://www.google.com/drive/apps .html#fusiontables and clicking on the Create link. At the Import new table screen, pick Google Spreadsheets. Select charting from your list.

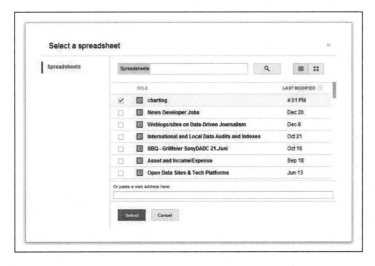

Source: Google Fusion Tables.

Note: Selecting a Google Spreadsheet for a Fusion Table.

First, we will create a line chart using the Pittsburgh weather data. Then, we will create a column chart using the GDP data.

To create the weather line chart, select the charting-PBGH Weather link, then click the Next button to import the table.

Source: National Weather Service.

Note: Importing Google Spreadsheet for a Fusion Table.

In the next screen, confirm that the column names are in Row 1 and click Next.

Source: National Weather Service.

Note: Importing Google Spreadsheet for a Fusion Table.

In the final screen, we can add metadata that can help us and others understand what's in our Fusion Table. Instead, we'll just click Finish and our table appears.

Source: Google Fusion Tables.

Note: Metadata box for Fusion Table. Metadata are data about the data and are a guide for others.

Source: National Weather Service.

Note: Data imported into a Google Fusion Table.

Click on the red plus sign and then Add chart. We now have the beginnings of a chart on our screen. Change the chart type to Line chart.

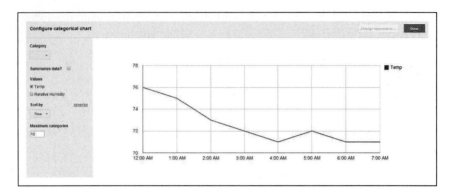

Source: National Weather Service.

Note: Google Fusion Table temperature line chart.

We're not done: we still need to modify a number of our settings. Under values, let's add Relative Humidity. Also, change Maximum categories to 26, because that's the number of rows we have in our data table. Much better! We're through, so click the Done button to finish.

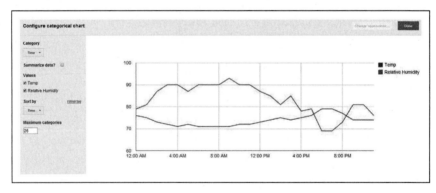

Source: National Weather Service.

Note: Relative humidity data added to line chart.

Now we'll create a column chart for the GDP quarterly change, which will be just a little more complicated. Return to your Drive and select Create, then Fusion Table. (If that option is missing, select Connect more apps and then search for it.) Go through the same steps as above to select the charting spreadsheet and then import charting-GDP. We now have this at the top of our screen:

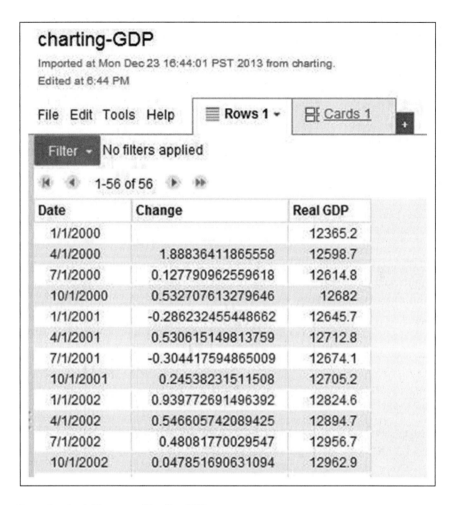

charting-GDP

Imported at Mon Dec 23 16:44:01 PST 2013 from charting.
Edited at 6:44 PM

File Edit Tools Help   ≣ Rows 1 ▾   ⊟ Cards 1   ⊞

Filter ▾ No filters applied

⏮ ◀   1-56 of 56   ▶ ⏭

Date	Change	Real GDP
1/1/2000		12365.2
4/1/2000	1.88836411865558	12598.7
7/1/2000	0.127790962559618	12614.8
10/1/2000	0.532707613279646	12682
1/1/2001	-0.286232455448662	12645.7
4/1/2001	0.530615149813759	12712.8
7/1/2001	-0.304417594865009	12674.1
10/1/2001	0.24538231511508	12705.2
1/1/2002	0.939772691496392	12824.6
4/1/2002	0.546605742089425	12894.7
7/1/2002	0.48081770029547	12956.7
10/1/2002	0.047851690631094	12962.9

Source: Department of Commerce, retrieved from FRED.

Note: GDP data in a Google Fusion Table.

We want to display only the results from 2004 on, so click on Filter and then Date. Filtering boxes appear. Enter "2004" in the first box and click Enter to display from that time on. Now we're ready to create the chart. Click on the plus sign and then select Add chart.

Pick Column chart from the options. Enter 40 into Maximum categories box, because we have 40 rows in our table. Click Done and we have our chart.

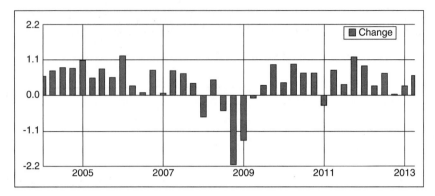

Source: Department of Commerce, retrieved from FRED.

Note: Google Fusion Table vertical column chart of GDP change.

Let's do one more thing: generate an embed code that we could use to post this on a blog or other website. Select Tools in the menu and then Publish. . . . This generates some HTML code that we could copy and paste. Of course, we would need to change our settings for the Fusion Table to Public for this code to work properly.

Source: Google Fusion Tables.

Note: Embed code for Google Fusion Table chart.

This chapter concludes the data visualization section of the book. As we saw above, it is pretty simple to create interactive charts using Web visualization tools like Google Fusion Tables. This is just an introduction to quickly creating basic charts.

ON YOUR OWN

Find data that you can upload to a Google Spreadsheet and use them to create a Fusion Table chart. Include the URL to the chart and a brief explanation of why you chose this particular chart style for your visualization.

CHAPTER 15 **TAKING ANALYSIS TO THE NEXT LEVEL**

A t this point in the book, we have achieved all of our goals for navigating the world of data. We have learned how to identify, obtain, evaluate and clean data. We've learned how to analyze and visualize them. Indeed, we've covered a lot of ground in the previous 14 chapters. We've accomplished these goals using software that's widely available and easy for novices to grasp. It really is eye-opening to see what we can do with these tools.

However, if we want to elevate our data analysis and visualization, we will need to learn more. Most people who analyze and visualize data use more than spreadsheets. They also use programs like database managers and statistical software. Here, we'll take a cursory look at these programs and how they can help us understand data even better.

DATABASE MANAGERS

Database managers, such as Microsoft Access and the open source MySQL, are designed to work with large files. Some database programs can easily work with millions of rows of data, something that's impossible with Excel's default installation settings. (Windows users can install an Excel Add-On called PowerPivot, which extends the program's capabilities.)

For Access, which is probably installed on the Windows computers in your campus' computer labs, the program file size limit officially is 2 GB. However, the program will start running erratically when the file size nears 1.5 GB.

Other database managers are more forgiving. In MySQL, a table may have 2 GB to 16 terabytes (each terabyte has 1,000 GB). Databases may have more than one table, so the file sizes can be huge.

Many database programs use Structured Query Language to issue commands. Developed in the 1970s, SQL is a powerful, yet relatively simple, database language that's taught in university computer science classes.

Some database programs, such as Access, also allow users to build queries using a **graphical user interface**. These GUIs make query building much easier than writing SQL. Unfortunately, they also deter users from discovering the benefits of learning SQL code.

There are some good arguments in favor of learning SQL. First, anyone who learns SQL on one database manager can apply that knowledge to another. So if we learn SQL on Access, it would be easy to write queries in MySQL with just some minor modifications. Second, anyone who learns SQL can talk intelligently to database administrators in government agencies, making it easier to negotiate for offline data. Third, learning SQL forces database users to think logically about their data and how they are structured.

Database managers are usually relational; that is, they allow us to create relationships between the tables in our databases. This is important because database administrators in government agencies often store data in multiple tables.

Database managers are especially powerful because they allow us to extract specific pieces of data that interest us. For example, using a database manager and the Federal Election Commission campaign contribution data we could find all the contributions to Barack Obama or Mitt Romney that came from our zip code in the week before the November 2012 general election. Another example: we could select records of high-potency (90 percent or greater) meth samples in the STRIDE data from the Drug Enforcement Administration. Here's a look at the STRIDE data, as imported to Microsoft Access.

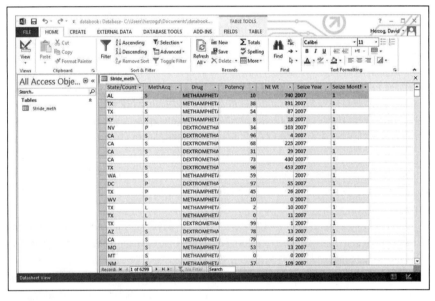

Source: Drug Enforcement Administration.

Note: Meth seizure data shown in Microsoft Access. Access is a Windows-based desktop database manager.

If we run the following SQL code, Access returns only those records where the potency is 90 percent or greater.

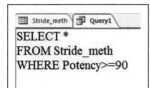

Source: Microsoft Access 2013.

Note: SQL to retrieve data about meth that's 90 percent potent or greater.

State/Count ▾	MethAcq ▾	Drug ▾	Potency ▾	Nt Wt ▾	Seize Year ▾	Seize Month ▾
CA	S	DEXTROMETHA	96	4	2007	1
TX	S	DEXTROMETHA	96	453	2007	1
DC	P	DEXTROMETHA	97	55	2007	1
TX	L	DEXTROMETHA	99	1	2007	1
AZ	S	DEXTROMETHA	93	1	2007	1
CA	S	DEXTROMETHA	90	14	2007	1
LA	S	DEXTROMETHA	96	0	2007	1
TX	S	DEXTROMETHA	95	0	2007	1
TX	S	DEXTROMETHA	96		2007	1
CA	S	DEXTROMETHA	99	0	2007	1
CA	S	DEXTROMETHA	97	3	2007	1
CA	S	DEXTROMETHA	96	74	2007	1
TX	G	DEXTROMETHA	97	2	2007	1
OR	X	METHAMPHET/	98	28	2007	1
CA	P	DEXTROMETHA	99	111	2007	1
WA	P	DEXTROMETHA	92	111	2007	1
DC	P	DEXTROMETHA	98	14	2007	1
CA	G	DEXTROMETHA	100	1	2007	1
CA	S	DEXTROMETHA	96		2007	1
MO	S	DEXTROMETHA	92		2007	1
CA	S	DEXTROMETHA	98	1	2007	1
CA	S	DEXTROMETHA	97	1	2007	1
CA	S	DEXTROMETHA	96		2007	1
CA	S	DEXTROMETHA	100	2	2007	1
CA	S	DEXTROMETHA	92	2	2007	1

Record: I◄ ◄ 1 of 862 ► ►I ►□ No Filter Search

Source: Drug Enforcement Administration.

Note: Query results showing meth that's 90 percent potent or greater.

Database managers are also great tools for grouping and summarizing data. They allow us to generate results that are similar to pivot tables. For instance, we could use grouping and summarizing to answer this question: Which state had the greatest number of meth seizures? This SQL code generates the answer: California, with 1,385 seizures in 2007.

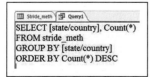

Source: Microsoft Access 2013.

Note: SQL for grouping and summarizing.

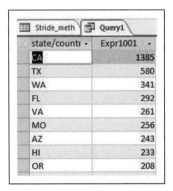

state/counti ▾	Expr1001 ▾
CA	1385
TX	580
WA	341
FL	292
VA	261
MO	256
AZ	243
HI	233
OR	208

Source: Drug Enforcement Administration.

Note: Grouped and summarized results, similar to those in a pivot table.

Data analysts often use database managers to create grouped and summarized reports like this.

Finally, database managers allow us to link tables together through a process called joining. So, if we get a database from a government agency that's stored in more than one table, we can stitch the data back together to better make sense of it.

We can see that database managers are very powerful programs that afford a lot of flexibility for data analysts.

STATISTICAL PROGRAMS

Though Excel has some statistical functions that can be activated with the Analysis Toolpak add-in program, most advanced data analysts prefer to use more robust standalone statistical programs, such as IBM's SPSS, SAS or the open source R. Statistical programs can easily generate a bunch of descriptive statistics, such as minimum, maximum, mean, median, count and sum. They can all run tests that allow us to see whether there's any statistical relationship between variables. These are called inferential statistics.

Some statistics programs, like SPSS, have GUIs that make generating statistics pretty simple. However, it can be difficult to understand the output and determine whether the results are meaningful, or statistically significant.

In this example using SPSS to analyze the STRIDE data, the author has created a **histogram** that shows the values for potency. A histogram is a chart that shows the distribution

Source: Drug Enforcement Administration.

Note: Meth seizure data in SPSS.

of values in a column. The histogram includes information for the overall mean, standard deviation and or count (N). The **standard deviation** is a statistic that reports how spread out the distribution is.

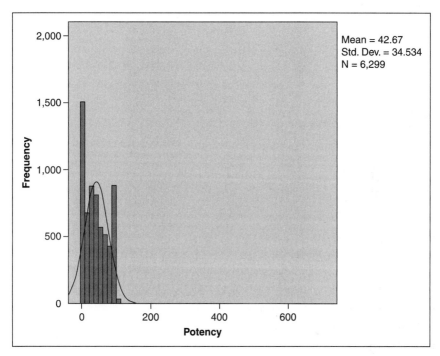

Source: Drug Enforcement Administration.

Note: Meth potency histogram in SPSS.

In medical and social science research, analysts will often run descriptive statistics first to understand their data. Then they will run inferential statistics to test their hypotheses.

Mastering statistics takes time and study. Most universities offer a great number of stats classes, from the introductory to the advanced.

Novices can also read S*eeing through Statistics* by Jessica Utts (2014), or *The SPSS Guide to Data Analysis* by Marija Norusis (2011). Both take clearheaded approaches to learning stats.

Remember, though, that even if we do not step up to these more advanced programs, we can still turn data into knowledge using the tools and concepts explored in this book.

All it takes is a little practice and curiosity.

APPENDIX **DATA TOOLKIT**

A nyone who wants to work with data needs to have some basic tools: spreadsheets, text editors and data cleaner. These are the tools used in this book, along with some other options.

SPREADSHEETS

Microsoft Excel comes as part of the standard Microsoft Office installation for Windows and Mac. It's installed on most university PC labs, as well as on many student laptops. This book uses Excel 2013 for Windows.

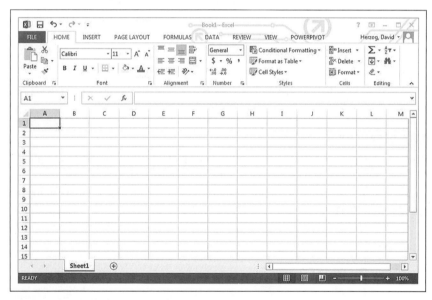

Note: Microsoft Excel 2013 for Windows.

Excel 2007 and later can open spreadsheet files with more than 1 million rows and more than 16,000 columns. Older versions of Excel (2003 and earlier) can only handle files with less than 65,000 rows and 256 columns.

More-recent (2008 and 2011) versions of Excel for Mac can open the same larger files as their Windows counterparts. Earlier versions of Excel for Mac share the same limits as their earlier Windows counterparts.

Another great spreadsheet option is the open-source program Calc. You can download Calc as part of the free OpenOffice (https://www.openoffice.org/) or LibreOffice (http://www.libreoffice.org/) software suite. Calc runs on Windows and Mac computers and supports large files (more than 1 million rows by 256 columns).

Google Spreadsheets might be a good option for working with smaller files—there's a 20 MB limit for files that are uploaded and converted. Furthermore, you can have only 400,000 cells. So if you have a spreadsheet with 40 columns, you are limited to 10,000 rows.

Pivot tables in Google Spreadsheets are primitive when compared to Excel or Calc. But Google Spreadsheets shine at handling live data feeds from the Internet and allowing you to collaborate with others.

TEXT EDITORS

Text editors allow us to examine our text-based data files. In this book, we use Notepad++ for Windows (http://notepad-plus-plus.org/), a free program. If you run into problems trying to open large files, you might have to use other text editors, such as the free PilotEdit Lite (http://www.pilotedit.com/) or the open-source Vim (http://www.vim.org/download.php).

For Mac users, the free TextWrangler (http://www.barebones.com/products/textwrangler/) and **TextMate** (http://macromates.com/) are good options.

DATA CLEANERS

We are using OpenRefine (http://openrefine.org/) in this book to clean data. OpenRefine is an open-source program for Windows and Mac computers. One of the creators of OpenRefine has said it should work comfortably with data files of up to 10 columns by 100,000 rows (Huynh, 2011).

Glossary

algorithm: A set of steps that a computer uses to solve a problem.

alphanumeric: A method of computer encoding that uses a mixture of text and numbers.

amount change: The raw change from one point in time to another. Formula: new number – original number.

ASCII: The American Standard Code for Information Interchange, which was developed in 1963 and is used to represent text on all computers in the United States. ASCII text is the most portable data format and comes in two main styles: delimited and fixed width.

.asp: Stands for Active Server Pages, Microsoft's scripting language. Web forms that have this extension use the script to pass data between the form and databases.

audit reports: Official reports that investigate the operations of government agencies. These reports can be used to uncover data held by these agencies. The U.S. Government Accountability Office examines federal agencies, while state auditors examine state agencies.

bar chart: Charts that display data using horizontal bars. Good for displaying data that fall into a few categories.

benchmarks: Points of comparison that help make data more meaningful. These can be internal—or within a data set—or external.

bit: The smallest unit of computerized data, literally a binary digit. Eight bits make up one byte.

cell reference: An address that refers to a cell's position in a spreadsheet, using the intersection of the column letter and row number.

central tendency: The average or number that's used to best describe a set of numbers. Averages include the mean, median and mode.

.cfm: Stands for Cold Fusion, Adobe's scripting language. Web forms that have this extension are using the script to pass data between the form and databases.

CKAN: An open-source Web portal that's used for government open-data platforms. Users include the federal government's Data.gov.

clustering: A function of data-cleaning tool OpenRefine that uses algorithms to identify similar text values.

column chart: Charts that display time-series data using vertical columns. Good for displaying events that occur at well-defined, discrete points in time.

concatenation: Merge two or more text values using spreadsheets or other programs. In Excel, the concatenation character is the ampersand (&).

CSV: Short for comma-separated values, a type of delimited ASCII file. Sometimes used as a file extension.

data: Any computerized file that uses columns and rows (a tabular structure) to organize information that's represented as text, numbers and dates.

data documentation: Detailed data description that allows users to more easily understand and work with data sets. Also referred to as data dictionary, record layout, file layout or metadata.

data integrity check: A systematic examination of data that occurs before the analysis; used to uncover shortcomings in the data.

data_notebook: A text or word processing file in which you record information about your data sources, as well as any data cleaning or analysis performed.

data portal: A Web platform used to distribute data; usually administered by government agencies.

database managers: Computer software designed to work with large data sets that are stored in multiple tables. Examples include Microsoft Access and the open-source MySQL.

dBASE: A popular database file format used by a number of commercial database manager programs.

decennial census: An attempt to count every person in the United States that takes place every 10 years, those years ending with a "0." The most recent decennial census was in 2010.

delimited text: An ASCII text file that uses special characters to mark the location of column breaks.

delimiters: ASCII characters that are used to mark the location of column breaks. Commas and tabs are the most common, but others can be used.

Drivers Privacy Protection Act: Passed in 1994, the DPPA is a federal law that restricts access to state driver's license records.

E-FOIA: Stands for the Electronic Freedom of Information Amendments. Passed in 1996, this law requires federal agencies to post on the Web lists of their major information systems.

embed code: HTML code that allows users to take content from external websites and embed it into their own blog or content management system.

exploratory data analysis: A systematic method for understanding data that relies heavily on charting.

Facets: An OpenRefine function that provides a list of all data values in a column and the number of times each appears. Similar to a pivot table in Excel.

Family Educational Rights and Privacy Act: Enacted in 1974, FERPA is a federal law that guarantees the privacy of student educational records.

file extension: The second part of a file name, coming after the period. Most file extensions are three characters long.

fixed-width text: A type of ASCII text file in which all of the data are arranged into columns.

geographic data: Data files that can be displayed and analyzed using geographic information system programs.

geographic information system: Computer program that's capable of displaying and analyzing geographic data. Examples include ESRI's ArcGIS Desktop and the open source Quantum GIS.

Government 2.0: A movement that started in the late 2000s that sought to use Web and mobile computing technologies to increase citizen engagement.

graphical user interface: A GUI is an interface that allows users to interact with a computer program visually.

Health Insurance Portability and Accountability Act: HIPAA is a federal law enacted in 1996 that makes personal health records private.

histogram: A vertical column chart that's used to show the distribution of values in a data set.

inferential statistics: The branch of statistics whose aim is to test a hypothesis about an entire population based on the analysis of data taken from a sample.

information graphic: Data visualization that is designed to communicate with a specific audience. Often created using design programs like Adobe Illustrator.

line chart: Chart that is used to display time-series data that are continuous, such as temperature readings.

linear regression: A statistical procedure that can be used to create a trend line for data displayed in a scatterplot chart.

mainframe: Large, powerful computer systems that can run more than one process. These computers, which have been around since the 1960s, typically are employed by government agencies and companies.

mean: The arithmetic average, which is calculated by adding a set of numbers and then dividing by the number of cases.

median: One of the averages. The middle number in a set of numbers that's ordered smallest to largest. If there are an even number of numbers, the median is the mean of the two middle numbers.

mode: One of the averages. The number that appears most frequently in a data set.

Notepad++: A free text editor that is capable of handling large files and showing hidden ASCII characters, such as tabs.

open-source software: software that is free in terms of cost and licensing. Also, the underlying source code is available to anyone who wants to examine or contribute to it.

open data: Data, usually provided by government agencies, made available at no cost and without restrictions on use. Often found on open-data portals.

open government: An initiative in the late 2000s that sought to increase government transparency, in part by making more data available to all, including Web and mobile application developers.

outliers: Extreme values in a data set. May be inaccurate.

parse: Carve out a portion of a larger text string. Used in data cleaning.

percent change: Used to express change in terms of a percentage. Formula: (new number − original number)/original number.

percent of total: Used to show individual portions of the whole. Formula: individual share/total.

Perl: An open-source programming language that is sometimes used to clean data.

PHP: An open-source scripting language. Web forms that have this extension use the script to pass data between the form and databases.

pie chart: A chart best suited for displaying proportions of the whole.

pivot table: A spreadsheet feature that allows users to generate summaries of data based on categories and numeric values.

primary data: Data that are collected by researchers. The data usually are collected from a representative sample of the entire population.

Python: An open-source scripting language that is sometimes used to clean data.

rate: A statistic that controls for population. Usually expressed in terms of a standard population, such as 100,000 people. Formula: number/population*100,000.

ratio: Used to generate a number that expresses the relationship between two things, such as a student-to-teacher ratio. Formula: student/teacher.

raw change: The amount of change from one point in time to another. Formula: new number – original number.

raw data: Data whose records or rows represent one person, place or thing. These data are not summarized.

records retention schedules: Documents that provide detailed guidance to government agencies about how long they should keep particular records.

Ruby: An open-source scripting language that is sometimes used to clean data.

scatterplot: A chart type that shows the relationship between two variables in a data set.

secondary data: Data that are collected by people other than ourselves.

servers: Not as powerful as mainframes, these networked computers are usually dedicated to one task.

Socrata: Seattle-based company that provides open-data platform services to government agencies.

sparklines: Small charts that are placed inside individual Excel spreadsheet cells.

spreadsheet programs: Computer software, originally developed for accountants. Spreadsheets store data in tables and allow users to run mathematical calculations.

standard deviation: A statistic that reports how data values in a column are dispersed.

standardize: To convert variations (often misspellings) of a data value into one correct value.

stock chart: An Excel chart type used to display opening, closing, high and low stock prices.

Structured Query Language: SQL is a programming language used to manipulate data in database managers.

summary statistics: Statistics that provide a snapshot of a data set. Includes counts, sums and averages.

text editors: Computer programs that are used to view and edit ASCII text files. Programs include Notepad++ for Windows; TextMate and TextWrangler for the Mac.

text qualifier: Optional characters that can be used in a delimited ASCII text file to denote text that should be kept intact inside a column.

Text to Columns: Spreadsheet function that allows users to carve data stored in one column into multiple columns.

TextMate: A free and open-source ASCII text editor for Macs.

TextWrangler: A free ASCII text editor for Macs.

time-series data: Data that are reported at different points in time. Discrete time series data are used to store information about things that occur at well-defined points in time, such as quarterly reports of the U.S. GDP. Continuous time series data are used to store information about phenomena that can occur at any time, such as temperatures.

trend line: An element of a scatterplot chart that shows the best fit of all of the points. Often based on a statistical procedure called linear regression.

visualization: A graphical display of data, created to help better understand it.

.xls: Excel spreadsheet file extension for original format.

.xlsx: Excel spreadsheet file extension for newer XML-based files. Introduced with Excel 2007.

XML: Short for Extensible Markup Language, which stores and transports data. Excel's newer file format (with an .xlsx extension) is based on XML.

zip file: A compressed file, usually having a .zip extension. Must be unzipped or decompressed before its contents can be used.

References

Ackoff, R. (1989). From Data to Wisdom. *Journal of Applied Systems Analysis, 16*: 3–9.

Agency for Healthcare Research and Quality. (n.d.). Medical Expenditure Panel Survey. http://meps.ahrq.gov/mepsweb/

Attorney General of Texas: Greg Abbott. (n.d.). How to Request Public Information. https://www.oag.state.tx.us/open/requestors.shtml

AustinTexas.gov. (n.d.). Dangerous and Vicious Dogs. austintexas.gov/department/dangerous-and-vicious-dogs

Awad, E. M., & Ghaziri, H. (2004). *Knowledge Management*. Prentice Hall.

Bureau of Alcohol, Tobacco, Firearms and Explosives (ATF). (n.d.). ATF Fact Sheet: National Response Team. http://www.atf.gov/publications/factsheets/factsheet-national-tracing-center.html

Bureau of Economic Analysis (BEA). (2014, Aug. 28). Gross Domestic Product, Second Quarter 2014 (Second Estimate); Corporate Profits, Second Quarter 2014 (Preliminary Estimate). http://www.bea.gov/newsreleases/national/gdp/gdpnewsrelease.htm

Bureau of Justice Statistics (BJS). (n.d.). All Data Collections. http://www.bjs.gov/index.cfm?ty=dca

Bureau of Labor Statistics (BLS). (n.d.). Mass Layoff Statistics. http://www.bls.gov/mls/

Bureau of Transportation Statistics (BTS). (n.d.). BTS Publications. http://www.rita.dot.gov/bts/bts_publications

Cairo, A. (2013). The Functional Art: An Introduction to Information Graphics and Visualization. New Riders.

California Department of Education. (n.d.a). 2010–11 Lorenzo Manor Elementary School Reporting Form for UMIRS Data. http://dq.cde.ca.gov/dataquest/Expulsion/ExpReports/SchoolExpRe.aspx?cYear=2010-11&cChoice=ExpInfo3&cDistrict=0161309—San%20Lorenzo%20Unified&cCounty=01,ALAMEDA&cNumber=6002653&cName=LORENZO%20MANOR%20ELEMENTARY

California Department of Education. (n.d.b). DataQuest. http://dq.cde.ca.gov/dataquest/

Center for Effective Government. (2013). Center for Effective Government Announces Launch: Press Release. http://www.foreffectivegov.org/center-for-effective-government-announces-launch

Center for Effective Government. (n.d.). Risk Management Plan (PRM) Database. http://www.rtknet.org/db/rmp

Chemical Accident Prevention Provisions, 68 CFR, Sec 68 (1994).

City of Houston. (n.d.). 311 Performance Dashboards. http://performance.houstontx.gov/311Dashboards

Coast Guard. (n.d.). Accident Statistics: Boating Safety Division. http://www.uscgboating.org/statistics/accident_statistics.aspx

Connecticut Office of Governmental Accountability. (n.d.). Freedom of Information Commission. http://www.ct.gov/foi/cwp/view.asp?a=3171&q=488272

Consumer Financial Protection Bureau. (n.d.a). A Snapshot of Complaints Received. http://www.consumerfinance.gov/reports/a-snapshot-of-complaints-received-3/

Consumer Financial Protection Bureau. (n.d.b). The Home Mortgage Disclosure Act. http://www.consumerfinance.gov/hmda/

Coy, P. (2013, July 18). The Rise of the Intangible Economy: U.S. GDP Counts R&D, Artistic Creation. http://www.businessweek.com/articles/2013-07-18/the-rise-of-the-intangible-economy-u-dot-s-dot-gdp-counts-r-and-d-artistic-creation

Cuillier, D., & Davis, C. N. (2011). The Art of Access: Strategies for Acquiring Public Records. CQ Press.

Department of Agriculture (USDA). 2013, July. Fiscal Year 2012 Farm Service Agency Farm Assistance Program Payments. USDA, Washington, DC. www.usda.gov/oig/webdocs/03401-0002-11.pdf

Department of Education (DoE). (n.d.). Family Educational Rights and Privacy Act (FERPA). http://www.ed.gov/policy/gen/guid/fpco/ferpa/index.html

Department of Health and Human Services (DHHS). (n.d.). Health Information Privacy. http://www.hhs.gov/ocr/privacy/

Department of Justice (DoJ). (1996). FOIA Update: Congress Enacts FOIA Amendments. http://www.justice.gov/oip/foia_updates/Vol_XVII_4/page1.htm

Drug Enforcement Administration (DEA). (n.d.a). DEA Major Information Systems. http://www.justice.gov/dea/FOIA/FOIA_TOC.shtml

Drug Enforcement Administration (DEA). (n.d.b). STRIDE Data. http://www.justice.gov/dea/resource-center/stride-data.shtml

Environmental Protection Agency (EPA). (n.d.a) Emergency Planning and Community Right-To-Know Act (EPCRA). http://www.epa.gov/agriculture/lcra.html

Environmental Protection Agency (EPA). (n.d.b). Risk Management Plan (RMP) Rule. http://www.epa.gov/oem/content/rmp/index.htm

epic.org. (n.d.). Drivers Privacy Protection Act (DPPA) and the Privacy of Your State Motor Vehicle Record. http://epic.org/privacy/drivers/#introduction

Federal Aviation Administration (FAA). (n.d.). Airmen Certification Database. http://www.faa.gov/licenses_certificates/airmen_certification/releasable_airmen_download/

Federal Emergency Management Agency (FEMA). (n.d.). The Declaration Process. www.fema.gov/declaration-process

Federal Highway Administration. (n.d.). Quick Find: Motor Vehicles. (n.d.). http://www.fhwa.dot.gov/policyinformation/quickfinddata/qfvehicles.cfm

Federal Reserve Bank of St. Louis. (n.d.) FRED FAQ. Economic Research. http://research.stlouisfed.org/fred2/help-faq/#graph_formulas

FileInfo.com. (n.d.). Data File Formats. http://www.fileinfo.com/filetypes/data

Financial Management Service. (2013, Sept. 22). Current Report: Combined Statement of Receipts, Outlays and Balances. http://www.fiscal.treasury.gov/fsreports/rpt/combStmt/cs2012/outlay.pdf

Food and Drug Administration (FDA). (n.d.). Total Diet Study. http://www.fda.gov/Food/FoodScienceResearch/TotalDietStudy/default.htm

Goldstein, J. (2013, July 2). Audit of City Crime Statistics Finds Mistakes by Police. *The New York Times*. http://www.nytimes.com/2013/07/03/nyregion/audit-of-crime-statistics-finds-mistakes-by-police.html

Government Printing Office (GPO). (2001a). State Numbering and Casualty Reporting Systems, 33 CFR Sec. 174. http://www.gpo.gov/fdsys/granule/CFR-2010-title33-vol2/CFR-2010-title33-vol2-part174

Government Printing Office (GPO). (2001b). Vessel Numbering and Casualty and Accident Reporting System, 33 CFR Sec. 173. http://www.gpo.gov/fdsys/granule/CFR-2001-title33-vol2/CFR-2001-title33-vol2-part173

Gregory, S. (2013, March 14). Sunshine Week: University of Kansas responds to "Let's Break FERPA" letter. Student Press Law Center. http://www.splc.org/blog/splc/2013/03/sunshine-week-university-of-kansas-responds-to-lets-break-ferpa-letter?p=4945

Hickey, W. (2013, Jun. 17). The Worst Chart in the World. *Business Insider*. http://www.businessinsider.com/pie-charts-are-the-worst-2013-6#ixzz2WU7bwUlY

Huynh, D. (2011). Google Refine Tutorial. http://davidhuynh.net/spaces/nicar2011/tutorial.pdf

Inter-university Consortium for Political and Social Research (ICPSR). (n.d.). List of Member Institutions and Subscribers. http://www.icpsr.umich.edu/icpsrweb/membership/administration/institutions

Lohr, S. (2012, Aug. 28). I.B.M. Mainframe Evolves to Serve the Digital World. *The New York Times*. http://www.nytimes.com/2012/08/28/technology/ibm-mainframe-evolves-to-serve-the-digital-world.html?_r=2&hpw&&gwh=D08AE3D472E69C065942744D18AC8E11

Look at Cook. (n.d.). Where's The Money Going? Brought to You by Cook County Commissioner John Fritchey. http://lookatcook.com/

Marshals Service. (n.d.) Major Information Systems. http://www.usmarshals.gov/readingroom/titles.html

McCallum, Q. E. (2012). *Bad Data Handbook*. O'Reilly Media.

Merriam-Webster. (n.d.). Data: Definition. *Online Dictionary and Thesaurus* http://www.merriam-webster.com/dictionary/data

Microsoft Developer Network. (n.d.). Introducing the Office (2007) Open XML File Formats. http://msdn.microsoft.com/en-us/library/office/aa338205(v=office.12).aspx

National Center for Education Statistics (NCES). (n.d.). Publications & Products. http://nces.ed.gov/pubsearch/index.asp?searchcat2=pubslast90&HasSearched=1

National Highway Traffic Safety Administration (NHTSA). (n.d.). Who We Are and What We Do. http://www.nhtsa.gov/About+NHTSA/Who+We+Are+and+What+We+Do

National Security Archive. (2007). File Not Found: 10 Years after E-FOIA, Most Federal Agencies Are Delinquent. http://www.gwu.edu/~nsarchiv/NSAEBB/NSAEBB216/guidance.htm

Nixon, R. (2013, Nov. 8). Telephone interview with the author.

Norusis, M. J. (2011). *SPSS Statistics Guide to Data Analysis*. Pearson.

OpenMissouri.org. (n.d.). Egg Licenses. http://openmissouri.org/data_sets/51-egg-licenses

OpenSecrets.org. (2014). Most Expensive Races. http://www.opensecrets.org/overview/topraces.php?cycle=2012&display=allcands

Osborne, J. W. (2013). Best Practices in Data Cleaning: A Complete Guide to Everything You Need To Do Before and After Collecting Your Data. Sage.

Oxford. (n.d.). Data: Definition and Pronunciation. *Oxford Advanced American Dictionary*. http://oaadonline.oxfordlearnersdictionaries.com/dictionary/data

Pell, M., McNeill, R., & Gebrekidan, S. (2013, July 8). Exclusive: U.S. System for Flagging Hazardous Chemicals Is Widely Flawed. http://www.reuters.com/article/2013/07/08/us-chemical-tierii-idUSBRE9670K720130708

Public Law 109-8. (2005). Bankruptcy Abuse Prevention and Consumer Protection Act of 2005. http://www.gpo.gov/fdsys/pkg/PLAW-109publ8/content-detail.html

Rowley, J. (2007). The Wisdom Hierarchy: Representations of the DIKW Hierarchy. *Journal of Information Science, 33*(2): 163–180. http://jis.sagepub.com/content/33/2/163.full.pdf+html

Silver, N. (2012). The Signal and the Noise: Why So Many Predictions Fail—but Some Don't. Penguin Press.

Sinai, N., and Van Dyck, H. (2013, May 13). Recap: A Big Day for Open Data. http://www.whitehouse.gov/blog/2013/05/13/recap-big-day-open-data

Smith, E. B. (2013, May 2). Disclosed: The Pay Gap Between CEOs and Employees. http://www.businessweek.com/articles/2013-05-02/disclosed-the-pay-gap-between-ceos-and-employees

Snyder, T., & Truman, J. (2013, June 26). Indicators of School Crime and Safety, 2012. http://www.bjs.gov/index.cfm?ty=pbdetail&iid=4677

Socrata.com. (2014). Socrata Customer Spotlight. www.socrata.com/customer-spotlight/

Susko, J., Putnam, J., & Carroll, J. (2012, August 28). Bay Area School Safety Data Flawed, No Oversight. http://www.nbcbayarea.com/investigations/School-Safety-Data-Flawed-No-Oversight-165171666.html

Tavernise, S. (2011, August 25). New Numbers, and Geography, for Gay Couples. *The New York Times*. http://www.nytimes.com/2011/08/25/us/25census.html?_r=1&

Texas Parks and Wildlife Department. (n.d.). Hunter Education Outdoor Learning Publications. http://www.tpwd.state.tx.us/publications/learning/hunter_education/

Tufte, E. R. (1983). The Visual Display of Quantitative Information. Graphics Press.

Tufte, E. R. (2006). *Beautiful Evidence*. Graphics Press.

Tukey, J. W. (1977). *Exploratory Data Analysis*. Addison-Wesley.

U.S.C. Title 46. (2011). United States Code, 2011 Edition. Title 46–SHIPPING. http://www.gpo.gov/fdsys/pkg/USCODE-2011-title46/html/USCODE-2011-title46-subtitleII-partD-chap61-sec6102.htm

United States Courts. (n.d.a). Bankruptcy Statistics. http://www.uscourts.gov/Statistics/BankruptcyStatistics.aspx

United States Courts. (n.d.b). Chapter 11. http://www.uscourts.gov/FederalCourts/Bankruptcy/BankruptcyBasics/Chapter11.aspx

Utts, J. M. (2014). *Seeing Through Statistics*, 4th edition. Duxbury Press.

Westhoff, P. (2013, Sept. 8). Telephone interview with the author.

Wolfram Alpha. (n.d.). Timeline of Systematic Data and the Development of Computable Knowledge. http://www.wolframalpha.com/docs/timeline/

Yau, N. (2011). Visualize This: The FlowingData Guide to Design, Visualization, and Statistics. Wiley.

Index

About the Author

David Herzog is associate professor at the Missouri School of Journalism in Columbia, where he also serves as the academic adviser to the National Institute for Computer-Assisted Reporting. He teaches computer-assisted reporting (CAR) and data mapping to university students and professional journalists. He writes and speaks frequently about data journalism, investigative reporting and access to information.

As a 2010–2011 fellow at the Reynolds Journalism Institute, Herzog led the team that launched OpenMissouri.org, an online resource that lists data sets held offline by state and local government agencies.

Before joining the Missouri School of Journalism in 2002, Herzog spent nearly 15 years as a newspaper reporter and editor. He has reported for *The Providence Journal, The Baltimore Sun* and *The Morning Call* in Allentown, Pennsylvania.

He has a bachelor's degree in Radio-Television-Film from Temple University.

You can find him on the Web at dherzog.com and on Twitter at @davidherzog.

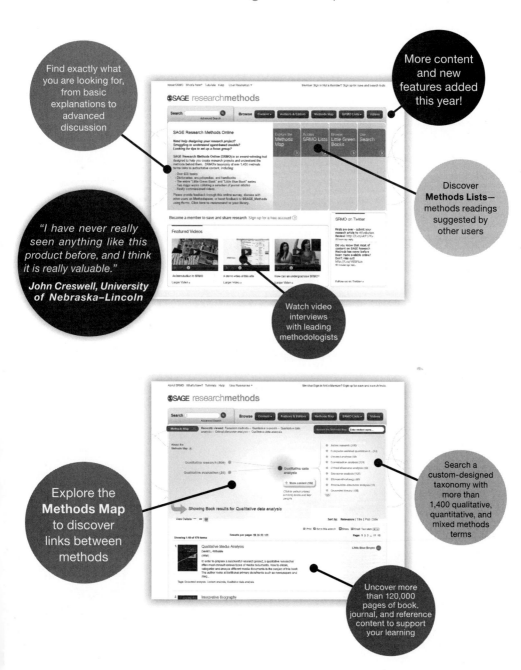

⑤SAGE research**methods**

The essential online tool for researchers from the world's leading methods publisher

Find exactly what you are looking for, from basic explanations to advanced discussion

More content and new features added this year!

Discover **Methods Lists**— methods readings suggested by other users

"I have never really seen anything like this product before, and I think it is really valuable."

John Creswell, University of Nebraska–Lincoln

Watch video interviews with leading methodologists

Explore the **Methods Map** to discover links between methods

Search a custom-designed taxonomy with more than 1,400 qualitative, quantitative, and mixed methods terms

Uncover more than 120,000 pages of book, journal, and reference content to support your learning

Find out more at
www.sageresearchmethods.com